Let's play together

Mildred Masheder MA, Ac.Dip.Ed. is a former primary teacher and lecturer in child development and multi-cultural studies at what was the Polytechnic of North London. She subsequently held a research fellowship exploring co-operation and peaceful conflict resolution with children and is the author of a number of books, including *Let's Co-operate*, *Let's Enjoy Nature*, *Freedom from Bullying*, *Windows to Nature*, and the play section of *Natural Childhood*. She has also produced a video on co-operative play and parachute games. she is currently writing a new book, *Positive Childhood: Educating Future Citizens*, which will be published by Green Print in 2004.

She has two children and two grandchildren.

Let's play together

CO-OPERATIVE GAMES
FOR ALL AGES

Mildred Masheder

Illustrations by
Susanna Vermaase

GREEN
PRINT

© Mildred Masheder
The author asserts the right to be identified as the author of
this work

First published in 1989 by Green Print
an imprint of
The Merlin Press Ltd.
PO Box 30705
London WC2E 8QD
www.merlinpress.co.uk

Reprinted 1992, 1994, 1997, 2003

ISBN. 1854250132

British Library Cataloguing in Publication Data is available
from the British Library

Printed in Great Britain by Antony Rowe Ltd., Eastbourne

To Marion and Susanna
who have given me so much love and support.

How the games are coded

Different games are suitable for different ages, and for varying degrees of activity. We have tried to help new readers to find suitable games quickly by using a simple code. After each game there are four circles or blobs: each represents in turn under sevens; juniors and young teenagers; adults; and those who are less active or have a disability.

If the circle is filled in thus: ● then the game is likely to be suitable for people in that category. If the circle is open, thus: ○ then it's less likely to be found suitable.

Thus a game marked ●○○○ is particularly suited to young children under seven, while a rating of ○○●● suggests primarily adults and a game also suitable for those who are less active or people with disabilities. If there is any chance of the young or the less active joining in *part* of the game, then they are given the benefit of the doubt and the game is marked as being suitable.

But categories like this can only be tentative; often you will be able to adapt a game for different age groups or levels of activity. Use the games we give you as a means of creating new games of your own . . .

The number at the end of each code indicates the *minimum* number of players recommended for the game as it is described. These are kept to the absolute minimum to accommodate where possible small families or just a couple of players.

Contents

broom Tableaux Charades Mime game Team mime
Miming rhymes Living tableaux Hand puppets Snake
charmers String puppets Give me your seat Passing a
gift Devil's advocate Opposite partners The seven
deadly sins Heaven or hell Acting proverbs Crises
Emotional statues Add your statue Strip tableaux
Hurrah! Assessment for clapping Petrouskas Funny
walks Take over

Construction games 61

Trust games 63

Nature games 68

Lively imaginative games 76

Tag games 84

Foreword

The young of all higher animals play exuberantly with one another. This has to be so. Play is not just passing the time, or practising adult skills; it is crucially formative. This is because more is going on inside the young creature than is visible on the outside: the vital neural networks upon which the fruition of individual life depends are being laid down. Many of these networks are the direct outcome of playful activities and relationships. This is especially true for young human beings because their process of growth is particularly complex.

An appalling error of the past was to suppose that children were being educated only if their energies were focused on a single aim: learning letters, or reading, or doing sums, or whatever it might be. But the educated brain is not unipolar but multipolar. The power of an adult mind is such that a single stimulus can stir the entire cortex into alert readiness and response. This elaborate system needs the right experiences to assure its growth.

It follows that whatever we organize to encourage children's learning should offer a *pattern* of challenge. One-track learning is dull and deadening; patterned learning is stimulating and exciting. Focused swotting can be of value only *after* lively motivation has been aroused by an appeal to the whole mind.

For this reason, the more one can build an element of play — of fun, of enjoyment — into learning experiences, the better the learning will be. Play is many-sided, provoking a whole range of educative interactions. The more exciting the play activity, the more it will arouse concentration which is the key to mobilizing mental powers and, therefore, to building the complexity of the ever-growing brain — potentially ever-growing, that is.

Whereas I have been lucky enough to be present in school classes in which liveliness and concentration have been magnificently displayed, I have also sometimes witnessed others in which most of the children were not at all turned on. These children were learning boredom rather than what they were supposed to be learning. It always surprises me that some parents who lose no time in switching off a TV programme that bores them, nevertheless expect that their children will benefit from being bored.

And, of course, it is not only playing as such that is educationally valuable but playing *together*. We now know that taking account of one another, in shared activities, is fundamental to intellectual, emotional and social growth.

So we must be grateful to Mildred Masheder for the encouragement and guidance she offers in this book, which help us to help the young — and those not so young — to become more fully themselves in the context of sharing fun and formative activities together.

James Hemming, B.A., Ph.D., F.B.Ps.S., F.R.S.

A playful questionnaire

Play is getting in touch with the child within us; to recreate ourselves in life. To understand it better, try asking yourself these questions.

What is play?

What is play for me on a daily basis?

Are there some activities that I do everyday that are sometimes pleasurable and sometimes not? What is the difference?

Has my capacity for play or experience for pleasure expanded or decreased during recent years?

What sources of play or pleasure have I not noticed in my life right now?

What play or pleasure do I reject?

How often does play or pleasure enter my life daily? weekly? rarely? never?

Recall the joyous times in your life; close your eyes and think. What do they have in common?

What is a source of joy in my life right now?

Do I honestly have a satisfactory balance of work and play in my life? If not, why not? Who is the wise observer in my life? Who is in charge?

With grateful thanks to Mrs Ludi How, counsellor at the Bristol Cancer Health Centre, who compiled this meditation on play for use with her patients.

Let's play co-operative games

The games in this book have two main things in common: they are all co-operative and are all played for the fun of it. They can be enjoyed by everyone, although for a given group of people some activities will be more appropriate than others. The spirit of co-operation is intrinsically linked with the idea of playing for the fun of it; in co-operative games all players find it mutually beneficial to help one another. It is a case of working together, making joint decisions and doing your best. So the challenge comes from the process itself rather than being the winner. This is in contrast to the vast majority of games and sports that are played today where competition is the overruling factor, so that the desire to win is the main incentive.

Of course winning makes us feel great, full of confidence and glowing with our achievement; but there are only tiny numbers of players who can win compared with the losers. They are always called upon to put a brave face on it, but it is hard not to be left with a feeling of inadequacy and failure. There are few people if any who have not felt a desolate sense of isolation at some time in their lives, and in our play we do not want this feeling to be reinforced and consolidated. In competitive games there is a great strand of elimination, and the words, 'You're out!' are constantly ringing in our ears. This can make many players feel vulnerable even though they are told that it is only a game. But when one is a child games and play are the basis of learning about the real world; the message is all too often that the world does not think too highly of you, and this can be the beginning of a poor self-concept. This is why we give special attention to games that will foster and enhance self confidence, which is the corner stone for getting on with others.

When we consider the major role that competition plays in our working lives, either at school or in our jobs, this seems to be all the more reason why it should not dominate our play — given all these implications for self regard and confidence. However, let it be clear at this stage that by promoting co-operative games we are not waging an aggressive campaign against competitive sport. There is plenty of room for all sorts of play, but there should be a greater balance between co-operation and competition, whereas at present it is completely unequal as competitive play has largely taken over. In any case there are not merely two extremes; all play has a great element of co-operation in practice: there must be mutual agreement on rules and in all team games and sport there is a tremendous group spirit which produces strong cohesion and mutual respect.

It is interesting to know that in many early societies there are well-established traditions of co-operative games that are played by adults and children alike. Human beings are by their very nature co-operative, although in our troubled modern world this does not always appear to be the case. In fact we could never have survived as human beings if we had not helped each other throughout our long evolution. In many cultures the very notion of competing against each other was a completely alien concept. In certain societies this still exists, although outside influences have been gradually eroding it. What still remain are the many co-operative leisure activities that have always been an intrinsic part of the culture, and these include not only games but communal dance, drama and song.

In our Western society also we have a rich heritage of co-operative activities handed down from one generation of childhood to the next. In many parts of Europe and North America they are still enjoyed in playgrounds and villages, but in recent years they have been declining owing to the drastic changes brought about by modern industrial life.

These traditional games have been well researched by Iona and Peter Opie in their book *Children's Games in Street and Playground*, and we find that they are still the basis for so many games that are played today.

The movement towards co-operative games that is so widespread in the United States and Canada has in many cases incorporated and adapted these traditional games as well as adding new ones, and this approach is rapidly gaining ground wherever it is introduced. They are now becoming well-known in Britain and are spreading rapidly throughout the country, and I hope that this book will be a source of ideas and inspiration to further this trend. It contains many of the established games that have always contained a strong element of co-operation, as well as adaptations of popular ones which replace the common practice of elimination — either by setting up alternative games alongside, for those who would otherwise be 'out', or by making the whole group the last one 'in' so that everybody wins.

It is harder nowadays to initiate these activities; there is the lure of television for adults and children alike, because of traffic or possible dangers of violence the areas are diminishing where it is safe to play, and the pace of life hastens the very process of growing up. It is all too easy to become passive spectators in our free time rather than creative and active players. It is worthwhile stressing how vital it is for children to develop through spontaneous and informal play; if as adults we missed out on this when we were young, that it is not too late to recapture it.

It is now generally agreed that the play lore all children received as their rightful heritage, usually from their peers and older playmates, has been essential to their social and moral development. They have learnt the need for structure, for rules that everyone must keep in an enjoyable and lighthearted way; in fact they themselves have been instrumental in making these rules. These lessons of sharing and give and take are hard for the younger ones as they naturally want to be the centre of attention and always to be the winners. If these attitudes do not change when they are emerging from this state to a more sociable and more democratic stage, it will be more difficult for them as adults to be as thoughtful and generous to others as we would all like to be. Of course co-operative play is not the panacea, but it can certainly help the new generations in a world that is increasingly depriving them of the sheer joy of spontaneous play.

On the positive side, if we do make the effort to try out games that are basically co-operative, it is certain that the feelings of goodwill and harmony that can arise will reap their own rewards. Whether in a busy household or a restless classroom or rebellious youth club they can bring a breath of fresh air. Children and young people are naturally disposed towards a playful approach to life and it does them good to share this with their adults, who have all too often put away childish things. It is well known that a period of relaxation will enable people to come refreshed to whatever task they are involved in, so a break for some spontaneous play can prove beneficial in any situation. I recall a rather intimidating meeting with some officials where we took ten minutes at the beginning to draw on a piece of paper three things that we were good at and then circulate amongst each other to compare notes and indeed to congratulate one another. The idea was not to include any aspect of their purely professional lives, and the result was a deeper understanding of the people they were dealing with and a much more productive meeting!

How to use this book

The book is divided into sections according to types of games rather than by age group. The idea is that people of different ages, abilities and energies would often be playing together and in any case both children and adults vary so much individually with regard to energy and inclination. To make the choice of games easier the more restful activities are found towards the beginning of each chapter getting more and more energetic towards the end. To a certain extent there is the same progression in the sequence of chapters, with the personal and circle games at the beginning and the more physically active ones such as Co-operative Sport towards the end. The advantage of the division into sections is that in planning a session or a party or a family pastime, one has a general idea of where to look and how to ensure a varied programme. I have played almost all of these games myself and I have found it helpful in organizing them to introduce contrasting activities, so that everyone has a taste of the wide variety available.

I have purposely not given exact instructions for each activity, partly because I wanted to include as many games as possible and also to allow for the greatest possible flexibility in their interpretation. Of course there are rules, but they are there to be changed by common consent if so desired; new ideas can be explored and completely new games can be invented. Children can expand their natural abilities for rule making and adaptation and adults can recapture creative powers that they may have forgotten.

I hope that all sorts of people will play these games, from toddlers to the elderly, from athletic types to those with disabilities. We all, young and old, have a child inside us who needs to be acknowledged and played with; it is a part of our intuitive and spontaneous nature and, by nurturing it, we can become more complete and fulfilled. There is no doubt that playing co-operative games together will forge bonds that will be long lasting and greatly ease the tension of our modern life.

Mildred Masheder

Choosing leaders and teams

Children have devised many ways of choosing individuals and teams that are free from favouritism or dominance. Their sense of fair play is apparent in the games that they have devized themselves or have passed down the generations as their own play lore, and they are meticulous in making sure that everyone has a turn.

Here are some of the ways in which players can be picked to be the leader or 'it':

The short straw   One of the players holds a number of straws or matchsticks for each one to pick. The one that picks out the only short straw is the one chosen.

Playing cards   The players are all dealt a card and the highest can be the leader, or the numbers can determine the order in which the players participate.

Counting rhymes   There are innumerable rhymes passed on by children to decide who starts:

> One potato, two potato, three potato, four,
> Five potato, six potato, seven potato, more.

The one who is counted on 'more' is eliminated and the count goes on until the last one is 'it'.

> Eena, mena, mina, mo,
> Catch an outlaw by the toe;
> When he squeals, let him go,
> Eena, mena, mina, mo!

A modern version changed from the old racist one!

Teams can be selected by everyone tossing a coin and then going to the side for heads or tails; if equal numbers are needed the larger team can keep tossing until it loses its extra players.

To divide a group into teams the number game of *Huggy bear* is ideal, making the last number the one that is needed for the game; or the leader can count round: 'apples, pears, oranges, bananas,' to get (say) four groups. To divide the players into two sides, one can go round counting 'odd, even,' in turn.

These are just a few of the many ways in which counting can ensure fair choices; any child will give other instances and rhymes. The important thing is that no one feels left out or is continually left until last to be chosen.

Personal games

Affirmations Everyone has a piece of paper and writes their name on the bottom and passes it to the next one, who writes something really nice about the person named on the paper. This is folded over and passed to the next one until the whole sheet of affirmations returns to the original player who can then read it. This causes a great deal of pleasure, and many people are known to treasure that sheet of affirmation.

○●●●3

What colour are your eyes? First everyone goes round introducing themselves to the others and saying 'Hello, I'm. . . .' Then after most players have met each other, they go round again. This time when they meet someone, they stay and look into their eyes for at least one minute. Then they describe in detail to the other one what their eyes are like, not just blue or hazel, but describing the various lights and tones. This is reciprocal; they then part and meet someone else.

○●●●2

Mapping Have a big local map on the floor. Each person locates their home, school and work place, sharing one reminiscence with the group. This can also be done with a wider range map where players can choose where they would like to be and why.

○●●●2

Transformations If I were an animal, what would I be? A fruit? An insect? A flower? What kind of animal, etc. Give your reasons and say what your life would be like. ●●●●2

Your favourite place Each one draws a picture of their

Mapping

very favourite place and tells the others about it; it need not be a masterpiece! ●●●●2

The senses Scent tests, taste tests, sound tests, touch tests, can all be a part of progressive games, where at each table there is something to do. With scent tests there can be covered saucers containing different things (like a piece of onion, or a sprig of rosemary). With taste tests, players have to be blindfolded and guess the taste of ginger, chocolate, etc. Sound tests can be with instruments of the orchestra, or more everyday sounds, for example, an apple being grated, or water being poured from the jug; alternatively, the noise of different articles falling to the floor is challenging — for example, a plastic cup, a spoon, or a book. ●●●●2

Aura Pairs face to face with palms outstretched with fingers upwards. The palms should be closely aligned to the partner's without touching, and each one can feel a warmth radiating from the two palms. ●●●●2

Shadows In pairs imitate what the other is doing. At first it can be mirroring as if one were standing in front of a mirror. As a progression there could be quite active movement such as running and dodging with the shadow always there.

●●●●2

True or false introductions People move about the room introducing themselves to other members. After the introductions each one should say two things about themselves, one which is true, and the other false. The partner has to guess which is the false statement and which the true one.

●●●●2

Lining up This can be a non-verbal game where everyone lines up according to their height, the length of their hair, or their birthday. A variation is to do it with eyes closed for the height and length ones.   ●●●●4

Getting to know you Here are a few ideas for warming up where participants do not know each other. Walk round the room shaking hands with as many people as possible and looking into each other's eyes at the same time. Move around the room again and touch the people you pass in an affectionate way.   ●●●●4

Interviewing Each player in a circle gets the chance of being interviewed by each of the rest in turn. They can choose a subject to be questioned on or simply answer questions about themselves.   ●●●●4

Struggles with a partner These mock fights can be very releasing: Yes no This is a purely verbal struggle with two people facing each other, one saying 'Yes' and the other 'No'. The tones can vary from gently persuasive to a shouting match!   ●●●●2

Elbow touch Each one tries to touch the opponent's elbow.   ●●●○2

Pointing match Each person points the right index finger in front with the left hand behind the back. The aim is for each to try to touch the other's left hand.   ●●●○2

Massage circle Everyone sits in a circle massaging the neck and shoulders of the one in front. Foot massage can be done in pairs facing each other. ●●●●2

Affirmative names In a circle each one in turn introduces herself by giving one or two affirmative adjectives beginning with the same letter as her first name: for example, jolly, jovial Jane, or handsome, helpful Harry. In small circles players can go round remembering each one's name and descriptions. The last one has the hardest task, but the group should help out. ●●●●6

The name you like Go round the circle asking each one what name they really like. Is it their own? Why do they like it? Then do the same for a job, or in the case of younger people, the job they would really like, and then the job that they wouldn't like at all. ○●●●4

Affirmation letters You write a letter to your neighbour saying three positive things about her or him. One trait can be physical, one mental and the other concerning the emotions; or people could be left to choose whatever they please. These letters are greatly prized by the recipients. ○●●●2

Three things I am good at Each player draws a sketch of what they are good at, apart from their job or professional qualifications. They then pin the paper on their front and walk round to see other people's drawings and talk about them in a mutual exchange. ○●●●3

Personal treasures Each player is asked to bring an object that they treasure most and describe why to the rest. ●●●●2

In common Everyone in the group wanders round finding out at least three things in common that they might have with other players, other than the purpose that brought them together. A variation is to give each one a list of ten items, material and abstract, which they have in common with any of the other players. For example, the list could contain such diverse items as a leather belt or a liking for New Orleans' Blues.   ●●●●6

My emblem   Each player has a sheet of paper divided into four equal parts. They draw four pictures: one of a time when they were really happy; one where they achieved something really special; one of what they would like to achieve; and lastly one of what they would like to be remembered for. Then they share their emblem with a partner or a small group.   ●●●●2

Mind reading   In pairs each person thinks of a time when they recall a wonderful experience, a terrifying experience and a peaceful one, which are labelled A, B and C respectively. In turn each player thinks of first A, then announces a change to B and likewise to C while the partner watches her face. Then the first player thinks of the three memories in any order and her partner has to guess which one she is thinking of.   ○●●●2

Circle games

Buzz This is a quiet number game where players count round the circle. When it comes to number 5 or any multiple of 5, they say 'Buzz' instead; when this is well established the number 3 can be added, when they say 'Fuzz'! If both 3 and 5 are involved as in the number 15, they say 'Buzz Fuzz'.

○●●●3

The parson's cat Round the circle the first one says 'The parson's cat is an angry cat' and the next one fills in another adjective beginning with 'a'; in between the group can clap their hands four times to give the player time to think. If, after that time, she has not thought of one, the next person goes on to an adjective beginning with 'b' and so on.

○●●●2

Back pictures The players sit in a circle, each one facing the back of the one in front. One starts by drawing with the finger an object on the back of the person in front of them. That person has to draw it on the next back and so on. When it gets back to the first person they tell the group how the picture started. This is really an artistic version of *Chinese Whispers*, when someone starts a whisper around the circle and it is repeated right round the circle. It generally comes out differently at the end, especially if it is a long sentence.

●●●●4

Wolf and rabbits Players stand or sit in a circle and pass a small ball around the circle one at a time. The large ball (wolf) is introduced and also passed round in the same direction. The idea is to try and get the wolf to catch the rabbit; when it catches up you can go in the opposite direction. It is more fun to introduce two rabbits which can pass each other if necessary to get away from the wolf. Each player has the chance to reverse the direction of the wolf by calling 'Turnabout' and then the rabbits have to turn at the same time as the wolf. Another variation is to throw and catch rather than pass. In this case the wolf catches the rabbit if it can land on the same person at the same time.   ●●●●4

Hidden bean bag One player goes out of the room and the rest sit in a circle. They throw the bean bag to each other until the player outside makes three knocks on the door and at the third knock bursts into the room. Meanwhile the player who has the bag has hidden it and the one from outside has to guess who has it. If only one knock is allowed then the bag has to be hidden immediately. This game can also be played by rolling a large ball to one other; this is more difficult to hide in time.   ●●●●5

Magic winks Sit in a circle and pass a card to each player, who looks at it and keeps it hidden. The Knave of Spades is the magician. If the holder of this card winks at you, you must leap up and freeze — the magician has hexed you and you can say nothing. People can try to guess who the magician is, but if they get it wrong they get hexed too. If you guess correctly the magician loses all power and everyone is unfrozen and the game starts again.   ○●●●6

Monster The monster is in the middle of a circle and is prone to attack anyone surrounding him. He advances towards a victim with snarling lips and claws ready to strike; if the victim can make eye contact with someone else that person can call out their name and turn the monster's attention towards themselves. And so it goes on. After a time, say six tries, the monster goes to sleep and another monster volunteers.   ●●●●6

Monkey One person stands in the middle of the circle and points to anyone sitting round, saying 'Monkey!' This player

Palm trees (see 'Monkey')

must immediately put two cupped hands over the ears and the players on either side each put one hand over their outside ear. If this is not done immediately, that player takes over the pointing. Variations are the well-known *Elephant* and *Palm Tree*. In the case of the elephant, the middle player is the trunk and the two on either side are the ears; whereas palm tree is depicted by outstretched arms straight up for the person pointed at, and swaying arms to right and left respectively. It's fun to think of other calls, such as 'Rhinoceros', with the horn in the middle and two little ears on either side. Mixing the calls quickly can be quite a game; for example, 'Monkey' to one player and 'Rhinoceros' to another. ●●●●7

Pass the smile The first player takes the smile off her face and passes it to the next one, who is looking very solemn until the smile is directed at her: she then becomes radiant.
●●●●4

Circle breathing The group lies face upward with their heads pointing to the centre; they shut their eyes and hold hands. They are to breathe in and out at the same time as their neighbours, at first breathing normally and then deeply in through the nose and out through the mouth. All their troubles are poured out with the rush of air.   ●●●●4

Roller ball   All the players sit in a circle on the floor and spread out their legs so that each foot meets the foot of a neighbour. One player is given a large ball which is rolled across the floor to be caught in someone's legs. The person rolling the ball calls out the other player's name, which is a good way of getting to know other people's names. The one who receives the ball can also be asked a question, for example, 'What is your favourite. . . ?'   ●●●●6

Hand bell   In a circle one person is given a hand bell with a clapper in it. She has to carry it across to someone else without it making a sound. This requires quite a lot of care. When she gets across she rings the bell and hands it over to the next player. The game repeats until everyone has had a turn.   ●●●●6

Little sister/brother, who is knocking at your door?   One player is blindfolded and sits down. Each of the others in turn taps them on the back and asks the question. It is a simple game of listening and guessing.   ●●●●6

Jack and Jill   Two players are in the middle of the circle. Jill has her eyes closed and tries to catch Jack by calling out, 'Where are you, Jack?' He then has to reply, 'Here I am, Jill'. She has one minute to catch him, both keeping within the confines of the circle. Then it is the turn of the next couple.   ●●●○8

The sleepmaker   Everyone sits in a circle with their eyes shut. An observer walks round the outside of the circle and taps someone on the shoulder once. That person is the 'Sleepmaker'. The observer then taps someone else on the shoulder twice, and that person is the 'Detective'. Then everyone opens their eyes. The Sleepmaker has to send people to sleep by looking at them in the eye and winking, but must do so without the detective seeing. The detective has to stand in the middle of the circle. If you are winked at you must pretend to fall asleep but not straight away. A more violent version of this game is *Killer*; instead of the sleepmaker, the murderer kills people in agony with a deadly wink!   ●●●●7

General post Everyone sits in a circle and chooses a town or a country. A player stands in the middle and calls out two towns or countries and these two have to change places before the caller can take the place of one of them. When the caller says 'General Post' everyone has to change places. A more modern version is *Fruit Salad*, when everyone takes the name of a fruit and it is played in the same way, the call 'Fruit Salad' being the sign for all change.   ●●●○7

Flowers and animals Two circles alongside each other; in one the players choose the names of flowers, and in the other, animals. When the facilitator calls out two names, one flower and one animal, each one has to jump up and run round the two circles without being caught by the other. If this happens, the one caught joins the other ring and chooses a new name.   ●●●○11

Twirl the trencher The players sit round in a circle and each takes the name of an animal or fruit. The first one spins a breadboard or an enamel plate and calls out one of the names chosen. Whoever is called must catch the trencher before it falls, spin it again and call out another name. Players take it in turn to spin the trencher.   ●●●○7

Chair share Players on chairs in a circle have been allocated into groups such as the names of fruits, birds, flowers, or trees with a specific name for each member. When a name is called, for example 'Banana', all the players in the fruit group move one chair to the right, and if necessary onto the lap of someone already there. This game could be developed by calling out how many places to the right or left players must move, and becoming quicker and quicker.   ●●●○12

Chair share

Detectives and thieves The thieves stand or sit in a circle and three detectives stand inside. The thieves have a bag of jewels which the detectives are trying to get. The thieves pass the jewels to and fro to each other; they cannot move and cannot keep hold of the jewels for more than 3 seconds. The detectives can move around, jump and pick up the bag if it is dropped. When a thief loses or fails to catch the bag, he changes places with the detective who has intercepted it.

●●●○10

Follow my leader In a new version of the old game, one person goes out of the room and the others pick a leader. The person comes back and stands in the middle of the circle. The circle has to copy everything the leader does, and the one in the middle has to spot who the leader is. This can also be played with free movement.   ●●●●7

Call, whisper and sing To start the game person A crosses the circle to person B and calls B's name. A takes B's place while B repeats the action to someone else, and so on. Then another chain is started by a different person, so that the two will be criss-crossing. With the second chain the

Follow my leader

names are whispered. When the two chains are going, a third starts; this time singing is introduced. If as sometimes happens one of the chains disappears, somebody must notice and start it again.   ○●●○**12**

Body ball pass Two circles are formed, the inner circle facing outwards and the outer circle facing inwards. Without touching it with their hands the players pass a beach ball round the two circles, keeping if off the ground. This can be done by rotating whole bodies as the ball approaches. If the ball is dropped then it goes back to the beginning. In another version the players in the circles are back to back, or alternatively, the circles can move in opposite directions (which can be easier). If there are enough players to make two double circles, they can each pass their ball to the other circle when the round is finished and again the ball cannot be touched by hand. There could be a friendly race between the two double circles.   ○●●○**12**

Spinning hoop The players sit in a circle. One spins the hoop and as soon as it seems to be going down, someone else must save it by rushing up to continue the spin. This is a popular pastime in China. This can also be played as a team game with two rows of players and two hoops. The first players set the hoops spinning, then run to a base and back to touch the next person in the line who has to get to the hoop in time before it stops spinning. ●●●○7/12

Bull in the ring There is one person in the middle of a closed circle of players closely linked together, and the 'Bull' is outside the circle. The game is for the bull to get through the circle to the victim inside while the rest try to prevent this. When the bull succeeds, two more take turns at being the bull and the target person. This is a more graphic version of *Let me out*, where one player tries to get into the circle while another tries to get out. ●●●○8

High and low Players stand in a circle and the one in the middle has a long thin stick or cane. If she shouts 'High', everyone has to duck down as the stick goes over their heads; if she shouts 'Low', they jump up as it runs round the

High and low

ground. It is confusing as high means go low, and low means jump high! It is best to have as light a stick as possible.

●●●○7

Elastic circle   Use a long strip of wide, very strong elastic and make it into a circle. Everyone gets into the circle and leans back so that they are supported by the elastic. You can feel the tension as you lean back. If you move to another position and let yourself be propelled by the elastic, the others have to move to accommodate you. Likewise if they move. After some practice it will be possible to move as a body in a certain direction.   ●●●○4

Traditional party games

Thus and so   This is like *Simon Says*, but the leader performs various actions, saying 'Thus does the policeman' (making traffic signs), or 'So does the guitar player'. If the remark begins with 'Thus', they must imitate the action, but not if it begins with 'So'. Those who do it wrong start off an inner circle, which will finally be composed of everyone.

●●●○**7**

Horns   One player is chosen to call out 'Horns, horns, bull's horns', and everyone follows the action of tapping the knees and then jerking the fingers up to the forehead at the animal's

Thus and so

name. When an animal is named that has no horns they keep still with their fingers down. Anyone getting it wrong makes up an inner circle, as with *Thus and So*.   ○●●●7

Birds in the air   Everyone takes the name of a bird. When their name is mentioned in the story, they flutter their right hand in the air; if birds in general are mentioned, everyone flutters both hands in the air.   ●●●●8

Fire, earth, air and water   A soft ball is thrown from one player to the next and the thrower calls out either 'Fire', 'Earth', 'Air' or 'Water'. If 'Fire' is called, the catcher remains silent; if 'Earth' she must name a land animal; if 'Air' she must name a bird; and with 'Water' a fish. If she answers correctly she becomes the thrower; if not the one next to the first thrower continues, and so on.   ●●●●8

Stalking   The hunter goes to one end of the room and the hunted to the other. The hunted has to get across the room to the other end without being caught. It is night-time so that both close their eyes and have to listen for the whereabouts of the other. As they are relying on their powers of hearing, everyone must be very quiet.   ●●●○4

Family coach   Each player is given the name of someone on, or something to do with, the family coach. The facilitator then weaves a story bringing in the various names (the coach-man, the mother, father, little boy, the baby, the whip, the innkeeper, etc.). When the players are named they stand up and twirl around and sit down. If 'Family Coach' is called, everyone must go through these actions.   ●●●●8

Monarch of the court of silence   The facilitator announces sternly that they are the queen/king of the court of silence. They command everyone to go and sit at the other end of the room. The monarch then sits on the throne at the opposite end and when silence is reached beckons silently to one of the people to come to her/him. That chosen person then has to walk without making a noise up to the throne. If the monarch hears them they are gestured at to sit down and someone else is beckoned forwards. The monarch must make strenuous efforts to hear if they are making a noise. If someone gets to the throne the monarch shows his/her pleasure by letting them choose others to approach the throne too. This continues until everyone is at the throne end of the room. This game is often followed by a group yell to release the tension of the silence.   ●●●●7

Murder   Each player draws a slip of paper from a hat. All the slips are blank except two, one of which carries the word 'Murderer' and the other 'Detective'. No one must reveal what is on their paper. The lights are turned out and the players scatter over the house. After a time the murderer chooses a victim, throws her arms around them and rushes off. The victim then counts slowly up to ten and then shrieks 'Murder!' The lights are then switched on and the detective takes charge. He questions everyone about their movements, and all must tell the exact truth except the murderer, who can lie. The detective may have two tries at picking out the murderer, but if she accuses the wrong people, the murderer goes free and everyone picks slips out of a hat again.

○●●○8

Vampires   Everyone is blindfolded and several are given the clue that they are vampires, by the facilitator tapping them on the shoulder. When a vampire catches anyone by holding them lightly at the back of the neck, the victim shrieks out and then becomes another vampire.   ●●●○8

Laughing game   The first person lies down on their back, and the second lies down with their head on the first one's stomach. The third one lies with their head on the second's stomach, and so on. The first one says 'Ha' whilst trying not to laugh, the second follows with 'Ha, Ha', the third one with 'Ha, Ha, Ha', and so on. This generally ends up in roars of laughter. You can try other sounds in the same way, for example 'Ho'.   ●●●●4

Poor pussy   One person begins by sitting on someone's lap and giving the most heart-rending 'meeows' to which the

Lucky dip stories

person has to say 'Poor Pussy'; this is repeated three times with the object of making the sitting player laugh. If he does, then he becomes poor pussy.   ●●●●7

Associations   One player calls out spontaneously a word, and the next says what that suggests to them, and so on, until a chain is built up. When each player has made three suggestions, all stop and try to work backwards through the chain without missing a link.   ●●●●4

Lucky dip stories   Various articles are placed in a bag. Anyone volunteering to tell a story picks three and weaves the story around them. There could be groups of three who share the story, taking one object each. Or it could be a spontaneous story with each one introducing his object in it.
●●●●3

Up Jenkins   The players sit round a table with their hands out of sight and pass a 20p piece from one to another until the facilitator calls out 'Up Jenkins'. All must then lift their hands with their palms towards them as if reading a book.

The facilitator can then order various movements such as 'drums' (fingers beating on the table), 'clap hands', or 'creepy crawly' (fingers and thumbs walking on the table like an insect) in an attempt to find out who has the 20p and in which hand. Once the command has been given 'smashums' (all hands smacked down on the table), three guesses are allowed in which to find the hand covering the 20p (in the old days a sixpence, and before that a threepenny bit!).

●●●●7

Sardines   One player goes to hide in a place large enough to accommodate everyone. As each one discovers the hiding place they squeeze up together and keep quiet. The last one becomes the next hider.   ●●●○6

Blowing the feather   All the players except one sit round a table cloth, which they hold tightly stretched. A feather is put in the middle of the cloth and the players blow it away from the odd player, as she reaches over to grab it.

●●●●5

Adverbs   One player is sent out of the room and the others decide on an adverb such as 'quickly' or 'crossly'. The player outside is called in and puts a question to each of the others in turn, and they must answer in the manner of the adverb. The questioner is allowed three guesses at the adverb. If wrong she is told and the next one in line goes out. ●●●●5

The priest of the parish   Players number off. One starts the game by saying, 'The priest of the parish has lost his considering cap and some say this and some say that, but I say number 3 sir.' (It can be any of the numbered players.) Number 3 replies, 'What, I sir?', 'Yes, you sir', replies the first caller. 'Not I sir' says number 3. 'Who then sir?' Then number 3 must reply with another number, for example, 'Number 5 sir'. Then it is the turn of number 5 to deny the charges and so on. If anyone makes a mistake or waits too long, he is then the one to be the caller.   ●●●●5

Categories   Players are in threes and take it in turns to be

A, B or C. A starts by saying a word, for example, 'train'. Then B has to indicate to C which category the word will go into: if he points his index finger upwards, the category has to be a wider one, e.g. 'transport', if it is more specific, he points his finger downwards, for example, 'Royal Scotsman' and if he points his finger horizontally it has to be another word in the same category, e.g. aeroplane. According to how he pointed C has to give an example without hesitation. A more complicated progression is to continue the pointing upwards, downwards or sideways from the last word.

○●●●3

Co-operative musical chairs and musical hoops We should bear in mind that many of the well known party games can easily be adapted so that they can become more co-operative and no one needs to be left out. For example, with *Musical Chairs* players can sit on anyone's lap, finally leading to the last one on a chair, or preferably with legs apart on a cushion and the others sitting lined up in front of her. Alternatively it can turn into *Musical Laps*, with everyone going round in a circle clasping the waist of the one in front of them. When the music stops they all at the same time lower themselves gently onto the lap of the person behind them. This is quite a feat and there is much jubilation when the circle remains intact. There is also *Musical Hoops* with a number of large hoops on the ground; when the music stops players have to get inside a hoop. As the hoops are withdrawn one by one, the players all have to crowd into one hoop, or at least have a toe in it. If there are no hoops available then pieces of newspaper do quite well with the facilitator tearing off pages or removing them systematically. Even *Musical Parcel* can have a final distribution of goodies for everyone at the end with the player who finally opens it being the queen and perhaps having something special as well, if the children are quite young.   ●●●○7

Dots Each player has a piece of paper and makes 20 dots in it and then passes it on to his neighbour on his left, who has to make a picture of a person, animal or object connecting all the dots. Then everyone guesses what the picture is.

●●●●2

Jigsaws   Everyone is given a picture postcard and scissors and asked to make a jigsaw of say 8 pieces. The jigsaw is then passed on to the player on the right, who makes the jigsaw, then mixes it up and passes it on to the next one, and so on.   ●●●●2

Hunt the thimble   A thimble is placed within sight of all the players, whatever height they are. Anyone who spies it does not give away the hiding place, but sits down quietly. The one to spy it first hides the thimble next time.   ●○○●4

Guessing games

Spot the changes   A variation of *Kim's Game* is to change the items on the tray. Which have been taken away? Which have been added? We can also do this with partners, changing something about our appearance secretly and then facing each other for our partner to guess the differences. ●●●●2

Questions   In pairs, one asks the questions and the other must reply truthfully, but not using the words 'yes' or 'no', and without nodding or shaking their head. When one says 'yes' or 'no' by mistake, it is the partner's turn.   ○●●●2

Deaf and dumb   The players are sitting in a circle and are counted round alternately 'deaf' — 'dumb'. The deaf ones ask questions to the dumb ones who can only reply by miming or gestures. Then they reverse roles.   ●●●●2

Mystery person   Each player has the name of a well-known personality pinned on their back. As everyone circulates they try to discover whom they are representing. They can try to find out by the way in which the others greet them and also by asking questions to which the answers can only be 'yes' or 'no'. When they have discovered who they are they can help someone else by asking questions with them, without looking at the label of course! When all of them have guessed their personage, those who would like to act out a scene as that person can do so to the rest of the players.

○●●●2

Labelling   Everyone puts the name they like to be called by in a hat. Each one then picks out another person's label and has to find that person and stick on the label. This can also be played with players writing what they would *like* to be; to identify the correct people can mean quite a few questions.   ●●●●6

No, you didn't The group chooses a leader who begins by saying 'When I went to the Himalayas, I found a . . .' (insert something here, for example, 'a waterfall'). While saying this the leader has to include some vocal or bodily action that the others have to spot. It could be scratching the nose or moving the feet. Each member of the circle has to repeat the sentence and include the extra action if they have spotted it. If they get it right, the leader says 'Yes, you went to the Himalayas'. If they didn't spot it, the leader says 'No, you didn't'. Each one has a turn at being the leader with a different sentence and a new action.   ○●●●6

Salutations One person sits on a chair at the end of the room, blindfolded. In turn players go up to her and say some kind of salutation. It might be 'Good morning, Your Royal Highness', and she has to guess the person from the disguised voice. After three turns of guessing wrongly, she gives the throne to the next one, who might choose to be the President, or the Emperor, and will make it known to his subjects.   ●●●●6

Guess the position Two people go out of the room while the rest decide what position they should adopt. It might be simply sitting cross-legged facing each other, or something much more complicated. As they get nearer to the position, the audience claps louder, or says 'warmer, warmer' until it is 'hot'.   ●●●○3

Mystery mummies Each team of three receives a roll of kitchen paper and two of them wrap it round the third, completely covering the body with the exception of the face. Then the 'mummy' is asked what sort of person she would like to be, and they proceed to make a mask to fit, also to draw on the paper the clothes that would be worn. Then the others guess who the mummy represents and who is really

Mystery mummies

underneath the bandages. Only one sentence is allowed for people to guess whose voice it is. Then the two others take their turns to be mystery people. ●●●●6

Squeak piggy squeak All the piggies are sitting in a circle and the farmer is in the middle, blindfold. He sits on a player's lap and says 'Squeak Piggy Squeak', when the player has to reply by squeaking. If the farmer guesses who it is, that person becomes the farmer. ●●●●7

World map This is a simple game I played with my father; just taking it in turns to find a rather remote place that your partner has chosen. Alternatively the name need not be given, but clues like 'hot and sandy, a town of three syllables beginning with T'. ○●●●2

Board games

Most board games have it as their main aim to beat one's opponents, whereas in these co-operative board games we play together and help each other to overcome a hostile element such as fires, hurricanes, and floods. Here either everyone wins or everyone loses, so losing does not make the individual feel a failure. Everybody is in it together, in the same boat as it were. Here are some examples from the German firm, Herder, which illustrate this point.

Fishermen   The fishermen live on an island. They own an attractive little boat which is anchored in the harbour. They use it to go out to sea to fish and they are able to help each other in hauling up the big fish which they could not do alone. Today they are rather anxious as they can see the thunder clouds on the horizon which will herald a violent storm. They have got to catch all of the fish before the tempest breaks, so they have to organize to co-operate together so that they can bring all of the fish back safely.   ●●●●

Adventure island   Four children arrive at an island and they decide to build a cabin there. But they need twenty logs to build it and there are none on the island. Each player will have to get five logs from the mainland. The players can help each other: they can go in twos to get the logs, they can give each other points which enable them to get the logs more quickly. Everything is going well until the sea starts to swell and it becomes more and more difficult to bring back the logs. What can they do?   ●●●●

Orient express

Orient express This is a race between a detective and an admiral, who wager that each one will get to Constantinople first, the detective by train and the admiral by ship. The players are to help the detective as vast destruction has been wrought by storms throughout continental Europe. Trees have been uprooted, floods have swept bridges away and undermined stretches of railway tracks. By co-operating to help the detective as they get points by the throwing of the dice, the players can get the train to Constantinople before the Admiral arrives in his ship. ○●●●

Other board games are supplied by the Animal Town Game Company in California. Here are several examples:

Save the whales Players must work together to 'save' eight whales while oil spills, radioactive wastes, catcher ships and 'floating factories' are moving them towards extinction. Players earn 'survival points' and make group decisions to try to save the whales. ●●●●

Dam builders You're a beaver, working with other beavers, collecting branches to build your dam, lodge and winter food supply. You must protect yourself from natural predators and the trap as well as from the Engineers. Beavers' work may be wrecked by flash floods, or a timber shortage or forest fires can slow down dam building. Conservationists try to stop the Engineers from building their own dam on the beavers' habitat.   ●●●●

Sleeping Grump   Grump has taken the villagers' treasures and is now asleep at the top of the beanstalk. Together players climb the beanstalk and recover their treasures, but Grump must not be wakened or he will take back everything. The players share the treasures and leave some behind for Grump. Their kindness will help to change him.   ●●●●

These board games can be ordered from the addresses at the end of this book. There is also the possibility of making your own co-operative board games along similar lines.

Artistic games

Head, body and legs This is similar to the well-known 'Consequences', where the first person draws a head on the paper and folds it, leaving the neck lines so that the next one can draw the body. Finally the next one draws the legs. A fourth player can add a title. ●●●●3

Interpretations Make a large blot of ink or wet paint on a large piece of paper and fold it in the middle of the blot. Everyone has a turn in saying what it is like; then the next player does their blot and passes it round, and so on. At the end a large group picture could be made incorporating the various blots, or each one could make a picture with their own interpretations. This could be an inspiration for a structure to making up a story: e.g. a butterfly, a gorilla, an aeroplane, and a baby! ●●●●4

Group mural Each one takes it in turn to contribute to a mural which is started by the first volunteer and then added to until the group feels that it is finished. ●●●●3

Fresco story Everyone takes it in turn to continue an imaginary story; they then paint a large fresco on wallpaper to illustrate it. ●●●●3

Guess the drawing One person has a long list of objects, e.g. a dog, a daffodil, a mirror, or a spade. Someone from a group comes over and is told an object from the list. They then go back to their group and attempt to draw it until someone in the group guesses what it is. Then the next person goes out and gets something to draw. Everyone gets a

Fresco story

turn to draw regardless of who guesses right. More advanced versions could be the names of pop songs or television programmes, for teenagers and adults. This could be a relay or players could go back to alternate groups; the first one to their own group and the second to the other one, and so on.

●●●●5

Double action painting With a partner, and your eyes closed, put your felt tips in the centre of a large piece of paper and move your pens round the page without taking them off. Go in all directions until you think you have covered the page. Open your eyes and make a picture out of what you have done and give your joint picture a title.

●●●●2

Tear away Using a large piece of newspaper, you are going to tear out the shape of an animal. In your group, decide on the animal you are going to make. Each person has one tear at the newspaper before passing it on. After a few goes try doing this without first agreeing on the object. ●●●●2

Double action painting

One at a time pictures One player is shown secretly a drawing or painting for half a minute. That player then draws it from memory and shows the picture to the next one for the same time or a little less. This continues until the last picture can be compared with the original. This is like the game *Rumour Clinic* where the same thing is done by showing a picture to the first person and each person in turn has to draw what is described to them orally. (If it is a sentence or two to be repeated this is generally played in a circle and is called *Chinese Whispers*.) In a favourite version of this game, you mime an action that is quite complicated, such as making a pancake, or getting up in the morning. The mime at the end can be quite a different action and participants who have had their turn can see the progression the mime takes.

●●●●5

Circle modelling A lump of clay is passed round. The first player makes a model of something and the group guess what it is. Then the second takes the clay and makes a different model, and so on. To be really imaginative, this can be done in mime without the clay. ●●●●4

Blindfold modelling In pairs, blindfold, sitting opposite

Blindfold modelling

each other with a mound of clay on the table between them, people can either decide what to model together, or they can just go ahead and see what their joint effort has produced. It is even more difficult to do it in silence, but very rewarding to discuss feelings afterwards.   ●●●●2

Code drawings In twos, plan a code for instructions for one to draw something simple that their partner has chosen. The code can be somewhat misleading, for example, 'up' can signify left, and 'down' right, 'home' can mean a circle. Various measurements will accompany the instructions and then they can see how near the original drawing they get. Half the fun is making up the code.   ○●●●2

Musical and rhythmic games

We've got rhythm One player goes first into the circle and invents a rhythm combining sound and music which everyone imitates. The next one goes into the centre, continues the rhythm, and then smoothly changes the rhythm and sound, which the others take over. This happens until everyone has had a turn and are all in the centre. ●●●●4

Musical circuit Everyone chooses a musical sound and passes it round at the same time squeezing the hand of the next player. This can also be played with simple musical instruments, but without the squeeze. Alternatively as the player is squeezed she makes her individual sound as though the electric current has caused it. ●●●●4

Musical hunt One person goes out of the room and the rest hide a musical instrument. When she comes back they sing a song, getting louder when she is near and softer when she is getting further away. When the instrument is found she is asked to use it in the way the group requests; for example, 'Play the drum triumphantly'. Musical instruments can also be used by the group, playing loudly or softly according to where the seeker is in relation to the hidden instrument. Home-made percussion instruments are generally used for this game. ●●●●5

Making an orchestra Everyone has a different percussion instrument and the facilitator asks someone to be the conductor. The music can start very simply and gradually develop to crescendos and diminuendos which can then be taped and listened to. There can be conversations between pairs of instruments; or one can play while the other joins in with movement to match the rhythm. Or half the group can play their instruments and the other half make up a dance movement to be in harmony with it.   ●●●●4

Musical lucky dip   Each player takes a musical instrument out of a bag, mostly percussion instruments. Behind a screen they play a few notes or make a particular rhythm and the rest guess what the instrument is. Then in groups they make up a composition to play to the rest with very simple rhythmic patterns. As a more advanced way of composing, each player makes a symbol of the instrument they have, for example a triangle will denote a triangle and a simple drum shape a drum; then they write or rather draw a combined musical composition on a board or large sheet of paper and play it. Again they can tape and listen to their creation! For the timing of the composition, a conductor will be essential, pointing to the symbol and to the player of that instrument.
○●●●4

Group yell   Everyone starts in a straight line, humming quietly and walking slowly towards the other end of the room. Gradually they get quicker and louder until on reaching the other end everyone is running and shouting. This can also be performed in a circle.   ●●●○6

Group hum   In a circle everyone crouches down and faces inwards. They start a very quiet hum, which gradually gets louder as they all rise to their feet in unison and then stretch their arms upwards. Then the process can be reversed, starting loud and slowly going down to a crouching position, getting quieter and quieter and finally lying down on the floor on their backs, feet to the middle in complete silence. A variation can be to chant all of the vowels in turn and then make a group chord with each one chanting a different vowel sound, if necessary with a conductor.   ●●●●6

Your move   In a circle one player starts with a simple rhyth-

Infernal machine

mic movement and the next one imitates it and adds another, and so on. The group is ready to help those who forget.

●●●○6

Musical freeze You can only move when the music (or drum) is played; when the music stops you freeze, and you take it in turns to call out how you should move — for example wearily, or chirpily. ●●●○4

Infernal machine Each player in turn becomes a part of an infernal machine, first with rhythmic movements and then added sounds. Machines could be musical, producing rock or blues with background tapes permitted. ●●●○4

Guess the song In turn each participant taps out a rhythm of a well known song or nursery rhyme and the rest guess it. ●●●●3

Dancing games Circle dancing is part of the tradition of people all over the world, and is usually accompanied by music and/or singing. The dances always involve linking hands in a circle; for example, in Balkan circle dances a typical hand hold is the 'back basket weave', in which the participants put their arms behind the neighbour's back and grasp the hands of the next person but one. When you lean back in this position you can spin very fast. Another harmonizing hold is found in French dances, where we link hands by joining our little fingers at shoulder height. Stories can be created surrounding the dance so that the movements form a kind of narrative; for example, the fire dance.

●●●○8

Mambo mamba This is a snake dance where everyone joins on to a long line holding each other's waists. They dance round in a snake-like pattern across the floor and get the rhythm of the music in their steps; at the last step of each phrase the head is jerked forward and you give a little jump. Other group dances of a similar nature are the *Cha Cha Cha*, the *Rumba*, the *Charleston* (in pairs), and the *Lambeth Walk*.   ●●●○6

Back to back dancing This is rather like mirroring, but

Silly dance

really dancing back to back. Other variations are finger and wrist dancing.   ●●●○4

Silly dance   One person gets up in the middle of the circle or carpet, and clad in a 'silly' hat begins a silly dance while the others sit round clapping and being generally encouraging. Then others can get up and join in and anyone can sit down at any time when they feel like it. Hats can be fabricated beforehand — one very successful one was a Morris dancer's hat decorated with ribbons and bells. This is a very spontaneous activity and demands plenty of goodwill and energy to be successful.   ●●●○4

Traditional singing games

Many of the traditional playground and street games were accompanied with singing and these are still popular with school children. They are constantly changing and different versions are sung and played in various parts of the country, in Europe and in North America. The ones described are all from my own experience in Oxfordshire, but they have their counterparts everywhere and have spread as far afield as the former colonies. The traditional music can be found in the Opies' book, *The Singing Game*.

Oats and beans and barley

Oats and beans and barley grow,
Oats and beans and barley grow,
Do you or I or anyone know
How oats and beans and barley grow?

First the farmer sows his seed,
Then he stands and takes his ease,
Stamps his foot, and claps his hand,
And turns around to view the land.

Waiting for a partner,
Waiting for a partner,
Waiting for a partner,
So open the ring and let one in.

Now you're married you must obey,
You must be true to all you say;
You must be kind, you must be good,
And help your wife to chop the wood.
Chop it thin and carry it in,
And kiss your partner in the ring.

This is an action song played in a circle with the farmer in the middle. For the first verse everyone skips round holding hands. Then the farmer scatters his seed, takes his ease by putting his hands on his hips, stamps his foot and claps his hands and then turns a full circle with one hand above his eyes to view the land. Sometimes all the players do the actions, which makes it more fun. The farmer chooses a wife in the next verse and she joins him and they twirl around to the last verse, which ends in a kiss. Then the wife becomes the farmer and it starts all over again.   ●○○○7

Draw a bucket of water

> Draw a bucket of water
> For my lady's daughter,
> One in the tub, two in the tub,
> Three in the tub, four in the tub.
> Four little dollies in a rub-dub-dub,
> Four little dollies in a rub-dub-dub.

Four players clasp hands in couples with one pair of arms above the other. For the first two lines they see-saw backwards and forwards, then they each get inside the ring in turn, by going under the joined hands of the players on either side of them. For the last two lines they jump up and down on the spot. This was a song accompanying the washing of clothes with the 'dollies' to toss them up and down.
          ●○○○8

How many miles to Babylon?

> How many miles to Babylon?
> Three score and ten.
> Can I get there by candlelight?
> Yes, and back again.
> Open your gates as wide as the sky
> And let the king and his men pass by.

The players are all holding hands in a line and the leader at one end sings the question, and the one at the other end replies. The leader then asks, 'Can I get there by candlelight?' and the other replies, 'Yes, and back again'. Whereupon the leader shouts, 'Open your gates,' etc. and the two at the other end join hands as high as possible and the 'king' then runs to the end and through the arch with his followers all in line with hands clasped. Then the position is reversed and the one at the other end becomes king. This game was sometimes played as a variant of *Oranges and Lemons* with the last one through becoming a prisoner; this gave everyone a chance of being king.   ●○○○**8**

In and out the windows

> 'In and out the windows (3)
> As you have done before.
>
> Stand and face your lover, (3)
> As you have done before.
>
> Follow her to London (3)
> As you have done before.'

This is an ancient circle game which had its origin in *Round and Round the Village*; then the village became houses, and the houses became windows. All the players join hands in a circle except one who remains outside; she weaves in and out of the arches that the players make with their arms. She should manage to cover the whole circle before she stops in front of the player of her choice. Then they both weave in and out of the arches and it all begins over again with the 'lover' outside the circle — so that everyone gets a turn.

●○○○**9**

In and out the dusty bluebells

> In and out the dusty bluebells,
> In and out the dusty bluebells,
> In and out the dusty bluebells,
> Who shall be my master?
>
> Tippitty tappitty on your shoulder,
> Tippitty tappitty on your shoulder,
> Tippitty tappitty on your shoulder,
> You shall be my master.

This popular modern version has replaced *In and out the windows*; the tune is different, but the action is very similar. The arches are formed by the circle of players and the one

In and out the dusty bluebells

on the outside weaves in and out while the first verse is sung. Then she taps gently on the shoulder of one of the players and they both go in and out with the tapped one leading. This continues until everyone is in the line; then the last one begins the next time round. ●○○○**9**

The big ship sails

The big ship sails on the alley alley oh,
 The alley alley oh, the alley alley oh;
The big ship sails on the alley alley oh,
 On the last day of September.

We all dip our heads in the deep blue sea,
 The deep blue sea, the deep blue sea;
We all dip our heads in the deep blue sea,
 On the last day of September.

The captain said, 'This will never never do,
 Never never do, never never do';
The captain said, 'This will never never do,
 On the last day of September'.

> The big ship sank to the bottom of the sea,
>   The bottom of the sea, the bottom of the sea;
> The big ship sank to the bottom of the sea,
>   On the last day of September.

This is probably the most popular of all the singing games; it has its origin in ancient games like *Threading the Needle* and *How Many Miles to Babylon?* which have the same format. The players are lined up holding hands and one at the end puts her hand against a wall. The player at the other end leads the way through the arch and, when the last one goes through, the one making the arch has her arm pulled, so that she turns to face the other way and her arms are crossed. Then the leader goes round in the form of a circle and leads the way through the arch made this time by the player at the wall and the one next to her. This process goes on until everyone's arms are crossed, all the time singing the first verse of the song. For the second verse the two ends of the line join to form a circle and they sing with their heads bowed down. For the third verse they wag their forefingers at each other and during the last verse they gradually drop down to the ground.   ●●○○9

Going to Kentucky

> We're going to Kentucky,
> We're going to the fair,
> To see the señorita
> With flowers in her hair.
> Oh shimmy, shimmy, shimmy,
> Shimmy if you dare,
> Round and round and round she goes
> And where she stops nobody knows.

This is a more cosmopolitan singing game which has been very popular in the 1960s and 70s, yet has some origins dating from the earlier part of the century when they dared to shake their hips in the 'shimmy' foxtrot after the First World War. Although the señorita is in the middle of the circle, all the players perform the actions as they sing. They dance round and show the flowers in her hair by making a circle with their hands at the fourth line. When they sing

'Oh shimmy . . .' they wriggle their hips and then twirl round and round with their eyes shut. When the señorita stops she still keeps her eyes closed as she points to the one that will be the next señorita. This is good as the choice is completely by chance and no one feels rejected by being left until last; in fact this procedure could be adopted in many of the choosing games.   ●●○○7

One little elephant

> One little elephant went out one day
> Upon a spider's web to play;
> He had such tremendous fun
> He sent for another elephant to come.
>
> Two little elephants went out one day
> Upon a spider's web to play;
> They had such tremendous fun
> They sent for another elephant to come.
>
> Three little elephants went out one day
> Upon a spider's web to play;
> They had such tremendous fun
> They sent for another elephant to come.

The players are dancing round in a circle and one is going in the opposite direction on the outside. She puts one hand on her nose and threads her other hand through the loop that is made. As they sing the last line she chooses another elephant who makes a trunk in the same way and becomes the leader with the first one holding on by her trunk. This continues until all the elephants are playing on the spider's web!   ●○○○6

Old roger

> Old Roger is dead and he lies in his grave,
>   lies in his grave,
>   lies in his grave,
> Old Roger is dead and he lies in his grave,
> Hey Ho, lies in his grave.
>
> They planted an apple tree over his head
> The apples grew ripe and they all fell down
> There came an old woman a-picking them up.

Old Roger got up and he gave her a push,
Which made the old woman go hoppity hop.

The last words of all the verses are repeated as in the first verse and then the whole line is repeated and 'Hey Ho' inserted before the final repeat in the last line.

Old Roger is in the middle lying dead and the rest surround him in a circle. They put their arms up high in the air for planting the apple and wave their arms up and down for the apples falling down. One of the players has been chosen beforehand to pick them up into her apron; then Old Roger gets up and gives her a push and the old woman goes hoppity hop out of the circle, and it all begins again with two different players.   ●○○○7

Drama games

Faces Who can make the funniest face? The most fearsome one? The ugliest mug? The most desolate one? ●●●●4

Partner sketches Each participant has a card with a personality described on it with certain definite traits. The facilitator gives the outline of a brief sketch and the players act it out in pairs according to their characters. Then each couple in turn gives their performance to the rest and although the theme is the same the interpretations will be very different. Each couple could also make up their own skit from the given characters. ○●●●5

Face masks

Face masks   Each person makes a mask of their face and then decorates it according to their taste. For adults the best way is to grease the face, put bandages over it avoiding the eyes, and smear on plaster of Paris. For children it is possible to use sticky brown paper without the grease and plaster. The masks can be painted and used for numerous acting games.   ●●●●2

Masked characters   Discuss with each participant what their character is going to be; they then design a mask to fit it. All then agree on a theme or a place — a circus, a seaside holiday, a variety show — and play it out spontaneously.
●●●○6

Temperamental labels   Everyone is given a label to stick on their forehead with a characteristic written on it, such as 'jolly', 'bad tempered', 'depressed', 'boring'. Players circulate and from others' attitudes towards them, they are able to guess their own personalities.   ●●●●6

Drama rituals   Each small group is given a theme: e.g. appearing and disappearing; greetings and goodbyes. These could be at a railway station or an airport, for example. Then each group creates a movement/drama around these themes.
●●●●6

Quick change actors   People walk around and the facilitator calls out characters like witches, Martians, cowboys, or spacemen. Each one has to face another and be a witch, or whatever. Then the music goes on again and when it stops there is the next call of 'Martians' and so on. Feelings can be added; for example, sad clowns, radiant ballet dancers.
●●●○7

Secret self   Everyone goes for a walk together, if possible through woods, fields or a park. Failing that, they find a space to themselves while they think of a hidden and secret part of themselves that other people rarely see. They then have to create a character out of their secret self. It might take the form of, say, an animal, an imaginary creature, or

Secret self

a sport. They start to move back and to rejoin the others and start to move and behave like the character, in fact to become the character on the return journey. Then in threes they choose a task or ritual or quest and perform it together, acknowledging each other's differing personalities, limitations and strengths. They can talk first if they wish, but it is better to get into movement as soon as possible. Then each group performs their movement/drama for the others.

○●●●6

Drama statues Someone chooses a person whom they model into a statue. First A chooses a person B who models A into a statue; then B chooses C who models B and so on. The last person may finish by making up a skit or small drama using the statues by making them come to life.

●●●●3

Group sculpture The players are divided into two groups. Group A designs itself into a body sculpture, while group B

Drama statues

goes out of the room. Group B comes in and appreciates what has been done and then creates a body sculpture within and around the one already formed, without touching anyone in group A. Then group A disengages and looks at the spaces now created and forms another sculpture, again without touching group B. This can continue for several changes and players can enjoy observing a creation as well as being involved in it.   ●●●●8

Family sculpture   Members of a family take it in turns to group a family sculpture together. They can also depict scenes such as the family at the seaside, the fair or the wedding.   ●●●●3

Hat tricks   Have a good selection of hats, and everyone chooses one to wear. They can go round the room to music acting what they think their character would be like, for example, a policeman's hat, a scout cap, a clown's hat, a bowler, and so on. There could be pairing and imaginary conversations between two or three personalities. A further game is when each one picks two hats and has a conver-

Hat tricks

sation, first being the one and then the other, for example a
football supporter and an army officer, or a fashionable lady
and a tramp.   ●●●●6

Telling your problem   One of each pair is told that they
have a problem and they want their partner to listen to it.
The other partners are told that they are very tired and find
it really difficult to be sympathetic. They then exchange roles
and see how they feel afterwards. They can choose any problem they like, using their imagination.   ○●●●2

Assertiveness techniques   In pairs, choose a conflict and
act it out three times with one person being constant in her
behaviour and the partner reacting in three different ways:
aggressively. timidly and assertively. One should bear in
mind that asssertiveness techniques are not aggressive, they
merely state the problem and assert their own needs. Afterwards they can act out the assertive method to the group.
                                                      ○●●●4

Islands   A group invents its own community on an island and plans the inhabitants and what they do, their festivities and customs. There can be action by the visit of peoples from another quite different island, perhaps of another group that has invented its own community. What happens when they get together?   ●●●●6

Picture stories   Take two photographs which have scenes with people in. Make up a combined story about them, each player having a turn to continue the story. Then act it out spontaneously.   ●●●●4

Family doll   A doll is placed in the centre of the circle and each one in turn says what relationship the doll is to them. It might be their grandfather or their sister, as the doll can be of either sex. They then say a few words about their feelings towards this relation. As it progresses the family relationships get interwoven, producing some interesting reactions and role play.   ●●●●4

What's my job?   In a circle one volunteers to mime a job, the others guess, the next one has a turn, and so on.
                                                                ●●●●4

Family doll

Contrary actions   In a circle someone starts by miming an action; the next one asks what she is doing and she replies something quite different. For example, she might be sweeping the floor, but she says she is playing football. The next one mimes playing football, and when asked, replies that he is tossing a pancake. And so on.   o●●●4

The magic broom   Everyone has to think of a job that they want to mime. The broom can be the prop that they can use for any purpose, except for a broom. Then the one who guesses the job is the next one to mime. Other props can be, say, a spade, a hockey stick, or a chair.   ●●●●4

Tableaux   Guess the subject that the other team is representing: e.g. the fair, the market, or a scene from a book — like Oliver Twist asking for more. A more active version can be done with movement in mime.   ●●●●6

Charades   This is like *Dumbcrambo* except that the word has a number of syllables which are mimed or acted out with speech in turn, followed by the complete word. The guessing team is told how many syllables there are.   ●●●●4

Mime game   Two teams, one in another room. Each plans a mime of their own invention; this might be simple (like threading a needle), or more complicated (like wrapping up a football to send by post). Then the other team, after watching the individual mimes, plans a composite story incorporating them all, although some will be misunderstood. Afterwards the two teams can compare notes.   o●●●6

Team mime   In turns each team chooses a theme to mime and the others guess it. It could be sports, jobs, or whole scenes like a circus.   ●●●●6

Miming rhymes   One player suggests a word, for example 'hat', and the others in turn mime a rhyme for that word, with the one who suggested the original word taking the last turn. Each one is guessed in turn and if the guess is not right the mimer can try again. This is an individual version of

Dumbcrambo where there are two teams miming the rhymes in turn.   ●●●●6

Living tableaux In small groups one is the sculptor. The rest will be moulded into a living tableau and the other groups guess what it depicts. In order to look at the other tableaux the groups will have to disband and then reconstruct their positions when it comes to their turn to be viewed. This is quite a feat of memory.   ●●●●6

Hand puppets By using their hands as puppets — as, for example, two people having a conversation — a couple can enact little dramas with great feeling. This can also be done by shadows on the wall where the usual donkeys and butter-flies can be made into a story.   ●●●●2

Snake charmers In pairs one is the charmer and the other the snake that gradually comes out of the jar and uncurls, and then finally does a dance. This can be done with shadow puppets, each cut out in cardboard, fixed to a stick and moved against a transparent screen which is lit from behind. Scenes can be improvised with great effect: we had a scenario when first a snake came out of the jar and then a mermaid, and they danced together in interwoven ecstasy!   ●●●●4

String puppets In pairs one stands on a chair and the other is the puppet standing with her back to her partner. She is really the one who leads the action. When the one on the chair manipulates the invisible strings, it is difficult to see who is leading.   ●●●●4

Give me your seat You try to persuade your partner to give up his or her chair or to open a fist.   ●●●●2

Passing a gift You decide on a certain mood — happy, sorrowful, begrudging, angry — and you pass a ball to your next neighbour as if it were a gift. Afterwards the moods can be identified and discussed.   ●●●●4

Devil's advocate One person plays Devil's Advocate and makes outrageous statements in a group discussion, such as

'Men are the slaves of women,' or 'I welcome the Greenhouse effect, there would be a lot more sun here.'   ○●●●4

Opposite partners You mime or improvise the opposite of your partner, e.g. rich/poor; tall/short; sad/happy. They can either agree beforehand or guess by acting the opposite of what the partner has chosen. A variation is to develop it into a conflict that gets resolved.   ●●●●4

The seven deadly sins Groups of seven act out the seven deadly sins.   ○●●●7

Heaven or hell In two groups, one acts out heaven and the other hell. When we did it, the ones in hell had a much better time than those in heaven!   ○●●●8

Acting proverbs Brainstorm lots of proverbs; in small groups choose one and act it out.   ○●●●4

Crises In small groups you are in a lift and it breaks down half way up; alternatively in a boat that has sprung a small leak.   ●●●●6

Emotional statues Each player has a turn in calling out a different feeling, such as weary, amazed, hopeful, furious, amused, cynical or terrified. The players make a statue of themselves in this mood for one minute, and then the next one is called out. When everyone who wants to has had a turn, they form small groups and make statues of changing states, such as dejection then triumph, obsequious then domineering, anxious then reassured. One minute should be allowed for each tableau with a gradual change to the other one.   ●●●●6

Add your statue One player starts by making themselves into a statue and the group decides on a name; then another joins and makes a statue relating to the first one and another name is chosen and so on.   ●●●●6

Strip tableaux Each small group devises a series of tableaux, which are then put together like a comic strip and the other groups can guess what is happening.   ●●●●6

Hurrah! In turn participants stand on a platform or table and are hilariously applauded by the rest. When this happened to me I was so pleased that I completely forgot to come down off my pedestal to let someone else have a turn.
●●●●4

Assessment for clapping Each one in turn gives a performance of clapping and the rest clap according to their assessment of each one. As this is a light-hearted affair, no one need be troubled by the assessment; in fact there will probably be the same sort of clapping for everyone. This game pokes fun at judging competitions.   ○●●●6

Petrouskas Everyone chooses a doll that they will be, and at night they all become alive as in the ballet 'Petrouska'. A situation can then be improvised such as a burglary or a fire. They could be at home, at a big store or waxworks. ●●●●5

Funny walks Each one in turn does a funny walk and the others go round imitating it. John Cleese made this famous.
●●●○4

Take over Two people improvise a confrontation: for example a tennis player and the umpire. Then a third person comes along and introduces a new conflict, e.g. a spectator protesting at the hold up. After that a fourth person joins in, e.g. a policeman arresting the spectator for being on the court. Finally a detective unmasks the 'policeman' who has borrowed the uniform to watch the match!   ○●●●5

Construction games

Faulty towers   In small groups, try to make a tower as high or as beautiful as possible with playing cards, dominoes or cartons. Then see who can blow them down with one breath, taking it in turns.   ●●●●2

Three ways to make an elephant   You decide what each group is going to make a picture or model of; for example, an elephant or a boat. Then each group is given different materials to use; one group might get glue, paper and felt

Three ways to make an elephant

tips; another a large sheet of sugar paper and paints; and a third various cardboard shapes and plastic containers.

●●●●6

White towers   In your group you have to make a tower as attractive and as stable as possible. You have ten sheets of A4 paper, ten strips of sellotape and a set amount of time. Use your hands and face to communicate as you are not allowed to talk. Take a minute to think up plans for your tower and then agree by sign language on one. The other groups' towers can be seen and admired after the construction is over.   ○●●●4

Bridge the gap   Make a gap between two piles of books and in a group you have to make a bridge strong enough to hold one kilogram or two pounds. You have paper, cardboard and sellotape to work with.   ○●●●4

Trust games

Leading the blind   Probably everyone knows this favourite game for pairs with one blindfold and the other leading. The leader can start by putting her arms round the blind one, and then progress to holding her hand and then only the tips of her fingers and finally, when she is really confident, letting go and directing her verbally.   ●●●●2

Blindfold walk   In turn each one walks the length of the garden or hall, protected by the rest if they go astray and when they finish.   ●●●●3

Find your partner   One of each pair is blindfold and they are directed by the facilitator to take so many paces to the right, then to the left, then forward. After a pause they are asked to find their partner by retracing their steps. To make sure they have found the right person they must identify them by feeling and touching.   ○●●●4

Human maze   Here one person is blindfolded and her partner directs either verbally or using agreed signals, e.g. one clap turn right, two turn left, three go straight on, and a whistle means stop. The rest of the participants form a human maze with paths to go through. They can be supplemented with obstacles if there are not many players. The maze can be stretched out by everyone holding hands. For young children a code of tapping on the shoulder might be more appropriate for the signs. A variation of this is when more imaginative scenarios are used: the guide can be a captain piloting his ship into the harbour; or an air controller guiding an aeroplane to land safely down a runway and taxi amongst other stationary planes to park. ●●●○**10**

True or false In groups of three with the blindfold person in the middle and the same human maze as before. One supporter tells the truth and the other lies so the blindfold person has to learn who to trust. With a human maze a wrong turn will not hurt, so this game should have no material obstacles. ○●●○**3**

Obstacle jigsaw In groups of three the centre one is blindfold and the other two link arms with her and have socks over their hands as they are not allowed to use them. All start off together at one end of a hall or garden, which have various obstacles to negotiate; at the same time there are pieces of paper with messages on which are to be picked up by the blindfold person. At the other end the messages are put together to form a whole; they can be phrases, lines of a song or poem, proverbs, or individual letters which can be assembled to make a word. ○●●○**6**

Care of the blind The group takes it in turns to be responsible for four blind people who need to be brought to the

Procession

canteen to have their meal. Other needs can be met, for example, a walk in the park, a visit to a strange house.

○●●○5

Procession Form two rows facing each other clasping the hands of the person opposite you. Each one in turn is carried slowly around as they lie on the outstretched arms. For strong people the one lying down could be carried above their heads. Alternatively, two couples could carry round a sitting person, perhaps crowned with laurels!   ●●●○5

Over the rollers As above, except the person is rolled down the line by manipulation of the supporting arms. They could choose between being on their backs or on their stomachs. Care must be taken when they are lowered down.

●●●○7

Caterpillars Several lines of five people, all blindfolded except the end one who directs the action by signs such as pressure on the right arm to turn right, or on both shoulders to sit down. In the end they turn into chrysalises by curling up into a ball. Then the inevitable — they slowly emerge as beautiful butterflies and fly round with the others. ●●●○5

Guessing the face Everybody wanders round with eyes shut and when they encounter someone, they explore the face and guess who it is.   ●●●●6

Trust partners There are a number of well-tried trust exercises with a partner: leaning backward knowing your partner will save you; sitting back to back and managing to get upright together; then going down again, which is more difficult.   ○●●○2

Trust balance Two people stand together facing each other; they put their hands out in front of them and move until their fingers touch. Then they lean forward slightly until their palms are touching and try to get the balance point. They can then rock very gently backwards and forwards. When they are more confident they can take a step backwards and do the same. Children have always used

Trust balance

partners to support them as they practise standing on their hands or heads.   ○●●○2

Partner see-saw   In pairs stand back to back and link arms. One leans forward and lifts the other off the ground and onto her back. After taking turns to do this it can be made into a rhythmic see-saw preferably with music to accompany it — or the nursery rhyme.   ○●●○2

Stage coach   This is an extension of *Horses* with four or six horses drawing an imaginary stage coach; there is a graceful ballet like this. If there are two stage coaches, they have to be careful not to crash into each other. A trust game can be developed from this with the horses shutting their eyes and being guided entirely by the coachman.   ●●●○5

Traffic control   This is the modern version of *Stage Coach*. This time with the driver's hand on the car's shoulders. With a bus, a train or even an aeroplane, the driver/pilot would be behind and manipulate a cord which would encompass all the passengers who would hold it with their outside hand.   ●●●○5

Trust circle This is probably the favourite of the trust games: a tightly knit circle is formed and a volunteer goes in the middle and with both feet firmly placed on the ground and body straight. She lets herself go so that the raised hands of the group support her as she sways this way and that with eyes closed. It is a wonderful experience and usually everyone wants a turn. ●●●●7

Nature games

These games are particularly important nowadays as so many people are living in urban areas and even for those living in the country there is not the free access of former years.

Nature Kim's game On a tray or cloth show a number of nature objects, e.g. cones, flowers, nuts, bark, seeds or stones, for 30 seconds; then cover them up. Can the group remember all of them? ●●●●4

Nature collage Everyone contributes to a collage made up of natural elements; it could be a miniature garden in a container with little rocks, pools, bridges and trees, or an expanse of ground for a temporary decor; it could also be a picture on the wall with stones and objects stuck on.

●●●●4

Jungle morning Everyone lies still on the floor. Imagine it is night in the jungle and all the animals are asleep. With the first light of dawn the animals stir, awake, they stretch themselves, yawn, begin to move around, to touch each other, to speak by roaring, whistling, snorting, barking at each other. We hear all the noise of a jungle waking up. Players could be given their particular animal beforehand or they could just improvise. The same activity can be centred round a farmyard waking up in the morning. ●●●●4

Nature hunt Each one has a list of nature objects to collect: e.g. an acorn, a thorn, a seed or a skeleton leaf according to

Guess my tree

the season. When they return they can make a nature collage
or miniature garden together. ●●●●4

Footsteps Look for footsteps on the ground, in sand at the
seaside or in mud in the country and decide whose they are.
Then imitate the creature, e.g. a bird or deer, cow or dog,
and the others guess what you are. This game can lead to
real trailing and finding as many different species as possible.
●●●○4

Guess my tree In a wood or park players sketch a tree,
then shape their body to look like their particular tree. The
others guess which one they have chosen. ●●●●4

Five senses Each person collects five natural objects, each
one to be guessed by the sense of touch, smell, sight, hearing
or taste. Except for sight the objects would have to be covered
or the players blindfold. An adaptation could be where each
participant in turn makes up a story, passing round under a
cloth items to be identified by touch. The story could mislead

by referring to a sheep's eye as a peeled grape is passed round. (Stinging nettles banned!)   ●●●●4

Looking up at the sky   My favourite inactivity, very much enjoyed by adults and children alike, is lying on my back under a tree and gazing up towards the sky. You can listen to the sounds of nature and just relax completely. The group can either choose their own space or surround a particular tree with their heads all resting near the trunk.   ●●●●2

Explorers   This is unexplored country and everyone collects specimens to take back home. What sort of a country is it? Alternatively each one has a list of things to bring back, e.g. a feather, smooth pebble, moss or fungus, according to the terrain. Everyone tries to bring back something really unusual.   ●●●●4

My favourite spot   Leading a blindfold partner to a special place that will be their 'cubby hole'; let them feel the natural vegetation around it. Take them back a different way, again

My favourite spot

letting them take note of natural objects on the way, making efforts to mislead them! Then they try to find their den and afterwards can decorate it as a sort of bower. Of course the other partner has a turn as well. ●●●●2

Bird spotting All proceed to a wood or place where a variety of birds are likely to come and count the number of different species that can be identified. They can be sketched and coloured for others to name. ●●●●2

Find your mate Each player has a picture of an animal, bird or insect and has to find a mate by acting the part and adding sounds. Two cards are needed for each creature and you need an even number of players. It is more challenging to mime the animal with no sounds allowed. ●●●○8

Animal jigsaw This is like *Find your Mate* except that you have a picture of an animal cut in the form of a jigsaw of two or three pieces. The game is to be able to spot what the

Turn into an animal

animal is from your piece and then go round to find others
of the same species by making the appropriate sounds.

●●●○8

Turn into an animal Either individually or in small
groups with the others guessing what you are: e.g. a tortoise,
snake, or mouse.   ●●●●4

Make an animal In groups of three or four choose an
animal and 'make' it with your bodies; the others have to
guess what you are. If it proves too difficult to guess, sounds
can be added.   ●●●○6

Nature treasure hunt The simplest form of this game is
where clues are placed in sequence and the first one to find
each clue reads it out to all the others. Finally there is a joint
treasure to be shared at the end; e.g. a basket of apples,
oranges or nuts. Examples of clues could be: a flower growing
under the old oak tree near the pond; or under the slide, or
swings in the park.   ●●●○6

Activity treasure hunt Here the clues ask for a number
of joint activities to be performed at each point, e.g. make a
miniature garden in the large plastic saucer, or make a collage
with flowers, leaves, twigs. The next clue would be given to
the group after the task was finished. This can be played
with several groups using different sequences so that each
one goes to a different task in turn. They can either add to
the previous creations, or better still, make one of their own.
These can be admired after the distribution of the 'treasure'.

●●●○9

Walk in the dark In a small group spot the stars and any
planets and listen for human, animal and bird sounds. We
are no longer used to walking in the dark, whether in the
country or the town, but we can recapture the wonder of the
night sky and the mysteries of the natural world. Adults and
children going together will make it safe.   ●●●●3

Night trek With groups clasping hands or joined by a thin
rope this can be an exciting adventure in a wood or parkland.

Night trek

The leader must have planned the trek beforehand and it should include some challenging feats; climbing over tree trunks, crossing a stream, clambering up steep banks slippery with mud. People can have torches with red plastic covers on them so that animals cannot see them. If there is a chance of seeing wildlife, then trekkers need to be very quiet. After such an expedition, hot soup or jacket potatoes can be enjoyed as people talk about what they have seen and heard ●●●○4

Trekking One or a couple have five minutes start and the rest have to catch them. They must leave an agreed sign every time they turn left or right, e.g. an arrow made out of sticks pointing in the right direction, or some knotted grass in the direction they are going to take. When they are caught, two more can have a turn and so on. ○●●○6

Animal dramas: Catcher and caught, Fox and chickens Two are foxes and the rest chickens. These games are great fun played in woods or parks where there are trees.

Chickens caught can change with the foxes, or help the foxes to catch more until the farmer comes and chases the two first foxes away back to their lairs. Variations could be bats catching moths, with realistic swooping and flying; or owls and mice. There is the possibility of the predators being blindfold; in this case the space has to be in open ground with boundaries, and some protection given.   ●●●○8

Wild animals   In an area where there is plenty of cover — woodlands, heaths, seaside — some people dress up as wild animals and go into the 'jungle'. When they're ready, they make their appropriate calls. The rest are each given three magic feathers which will make the animals run off, but when their feathers are used up they can be caught and have to live with the wild animals and help catch more children.
○●●○9

Hide and seek   The great outdoors is the best place for this ever popular game. There can be equal teams of hiders and seekers, or just a couple going off to hide. In each case

Hide and seek

when anyone is found they join the seekers; alternatively they can get back to an agreed 'home'. Another variation is that the hiders have to stay where they are when the seekers call that they are starting out. An old country game is where the seekers call out 'Holler Holler, or the dogs won't follow!'; then the hiders must 'Holler' to show their whereabouts. This is generally called *Fox and Hounds*. ●●●○6

Nature treasure hunt This is like the usual treasure hunt but all the clues are based on a knowledge of nature: for example, 'where the woodpecker likes to nest' when the next clue is in the small hollow of a tree. The final treasure should be in keeping: an apple or a bag of nuts for everyone.

●●●○5

For many more nature games and activities I would like to recommend Joseph Cornell's *Sharing Nature with Children*. It gives many really good games which are great fun, and also teaches us more about nature's secrets.

Lively imaginative games

The tiger and the peasants   There is one tiger who goes outside while the peasants work in the fields. Suddenly there is a roar: it is the tiger coming to eat them! They must lie down and act as though they are dead, even when the tiger shakes them to see if they are alive (no tickling!). Any caught can join the tigers or change places with a tiger.   ●●●○5

Sleeping dinosaurs   The dinosaurs go stomping about the place until finally they are overcome by sleep and gradually sink their enormous bodies down on the ground. The facilitator comes round to see if they are all really asleep and if they move at all they are touched on the shoulder and then they have to get up and spot other stirring dinosaurs. This is a popular variation of *Sleeping Lions*.   ●●●○5

Car factory   The players stand in two lines facing each other with some space between each couple. Each participant in turn chooses the vehicle he or she would like to become: say a Land Rover, a Rolls Royce, a tractor or a pony trap. As they go down the line each couple uses their imagination to add various parts, either in consultation before the assembly line starts or spontaneously. For example, the first ones would start with making the metal body and the last ones would be giving such finishing touches as the headlights. Young children will be happy to go off tooting their horns at break-neck speed! This is a more dramatic version of the popular *Car Wash*, where the car is sent down the line to be sprayed with water and polished. It is also like the well-known *Biscuit Factory*, where each player chooses a special kind of biscuit that they will be made into; for example, fig rolls, jaffa cake, or chocolate digestive.   ●●●○7

Circus horses   Half the players form a circle kneeling with their backs to the centre and holding out yard-long thin canes for the horses to jump over. The horses jump in line to music following the leader who will trot, canter and gallop. When the music stops the horses change places with the players holding the sticks. A more energetic version is where the cane holders climb onto the backs of the horses and become riders.   ●●●○8

Cobbler, cobbler, mend my shoe   Everyone puts one of their shoes in the middle of the circle and dances round to the nursery rhyme; at the end they all go to the middle and choose another shoe. This can be done blindfold. They then go round wearing odd pairs, with only toes in where it might be uncomfortable. At the call of 'half-past two' they try to find the person wearing their other shoe and stand so that the shoes are side by side. As the exchange will not be just

Cobbler, cobbler, mend my shoe

between two pairs of shoes there will be some stretching of legs and bodies to get each pair lined up. Then they slip out of them and get into their proper shoes without using their hands. One more complicated version is where both shoes are removed and everyone takes odd shoes not their own and then tries to match up the two owners. Again they have to shuffle round with only toes in the odd shoes.   ●●●○8

Sailors   This is a slight variation on an old favourite, *Fish Gobbler*. The group forms a single file along a centre line. If the leader shouts 'Starboard', everyone runs right, and if the leader shouts 'Port', everyone runs left. 'Shipshape' means back to the centre. The leader shouts commands faster and faster and people become quite confused. Variations can be added: for example, if the leader shouts 'Sharks', the whole group can form themselves into the shape of a huge fish which the sharks do not dare to tackle; 'Octopus' can get everyone clinging to each other as tightly as they can so that the tentacles cannot claw them!   ●●●○7

Where are we?   Played in groups of six standing in the centre of the room or garden. The four walls or four corners of the garden are labelled 'jungle', 'desert', 'ocean', and 'city'. The caller calls out the area and something suitable to that area: e.g. 'jungle — snake', 'desert — palm', 'ocean — submarine', 'city — bus', and the players run to that place and form themselves into the shape of whatever was called. A more advanced version would be to call out a shape without saying which area: e.g. camel, or monkey. Alternatively the area only can be called out and each group decides how they should represent it.   ○●●○7

Boats across the channel   Everyone makes a paper boat and all the boats are placed in a line in Dover Harbour. The Channel can be represented by a long strip of shiny brown paper a metre wide and a few metres long, or a roll of wallpaper. Or for a game with only two players, it could be the bath, and for a greater number a shallow pool. The players divide into three groups, one producing gentle wind, the second a more powerful wind, and the third gale force. First the gentle breezes are used to get the boats started by means of fanning with sheets of cardboard, then the stronger wind team can blow the boats along using their breath and cardboard sheets. The third gale force team are allowed to use breath, cardboard sheets, and funnels. The aim is to get all the boats to Calais without them falling over. If they do fall over, they can be rescued by the winds blowing two boats at either side of them. If all of the boats fall over into the 'water', then they are all lost at sea and the game can start again.   ●●●○6

Fire engines The group or groups all stand facing one direction and each leader points to a fire fifteen metres or more away. The fire engine leader goes first to put the fire out making a siren noise as she goes, taking out the hose and spraying the fire. It is too large a fire so she has to go back and get another fire engine, and so on, until the whole group have finally put out the fire together. This is a great favourite with young children.   ●○○○6

The Tube game Everyone sits in a circle on chairs or cushions and is given a piece of paper with the name of a

Fire engines

station on the London Underground and the line it is on. If there are twelve people playing in the circle then four lines will be involved; if more then there can be more lines. The controller is standing up and calls the name of one of the four lines. The people who have stations on this line have to exchange seats. The controller quickly tries to get one of their seats and if successful the one left in the middle becomes the new controller; they call out one of the underground lines, or, for example, ask for all stations with an 'a' in their names; or they call more than one line at a time and these people have to change seats and again the one in the middle gives the call, and so on.

In order to change the game, the leader, who was the first controller, has to get to the centre again, and she will stay there until the end of the game. She will call out that, for example, there is a power failure on one of the lines, and all those passengers have to sit on the lap of one of the people next to them. She can call out next that there is a strike on another line and the passengers on that line have to sit on the lap of the person next to them, even if there is already a person sitting on their lap. If you're sitting on someone's lap you have to move with them.   ○●●○12

Musical laps Players form a circle with hands firmly clasping the one in front of them. They walk round and when the music stops, they have to sit on the lap of the person behind them. At first the circle usually collapses, but after some practice they can manage complete equilibrium and even speed up the pace into a run.   ●●●○6

Catch the dragon's tail All but two players make up dragons of about four people, each clasping the waist of the person in front. One of the two extra players tries to tag on to one of the dragon's tails while the other tries to hit her with a soft ball. If the former succeeds in joining a dragon then that dragon's 'head' takes her place; if she is tagged by the catcher, then they change places. A simpler version is one chaser to each dragon, but any tail is fair game. Another way of playing this traditional game is for the head of the dragon to try to catch its own tail, and when it does the second person becomes the head.   ●●●○6

Puffing Billy   Everyone clasping the waist of the player in front and surmounting a number of obstacles: 'mountains', 'bridges', 'tunnels'. They chant the rhythm 'I hope I can, I think I can, I know I can' as they go through the various obstacles, with hoots at the approach of each one.   ●○○○4

Puffer trains   Mark out a large circle as a railway track with everyone standing round it. Two leaders are the engines; each starts from one point on the circle puffing round the outside of the players and coming back to face the ones who were originally next to them, saying 'Hello, what's your name?' 'Sarah'. 'Hello Sarah!' Sarah then becomes the engine and the two make the journey round the circle, being careful not to bump into the other couple coming in the opposite direction. This continues taking everyone in line until there are just two trains which could then join together and go round the circle at speed, hooting all the way!   ●●●○8

Horses   This is a traditional game played in twos with string tied to the 'horses' hands or arms to make reins. I recall playing at trotting, cantering and galloping until I rolled on the ground with a stitch.   ●○○○2

Cowboys and wild horses   Four players are cowboys and the rest horses. The cowboys have lassoes, each one with their own colour, and a stable, which can be a loop or a marked square. At a given signal the cowboys chase the horses and put a lasso round them leading them to their stable. When all the horses are caught the cowboys make up their teams with ropes and gallop them round the stables.
                                                        ●●●○12

Huggy bear   At the call 'Huggy Bear' players group according to the instruction given; 'Huggy Bear, two', or three, or any number. This is a very useful way of getting people into groups quickly and without any stress. (Shall I be chosen?) This simple method can be applied to other possibilities:

Huggy bear

'everyone of the same height', 'anyone wearing the same coloured clothes as you', or with the same colour eyes. It can also extend to things around the room or outside: 'Huggy Bear' anything made of wood or metal, something new, something lively, inanimate.   ●●●○8

Wind up the clocks   Everyone is a clockwork figure going through a series of actions. They run down towards the end and have to depend on another 'clock' to come and wind them up before they collapse.   ●●●○6

Looking glass   Partners start face to face and imitate each other so that their actions synchronise exactly as if they were in front of a mirror.   ●●●●2

Hominoes   People play this game like dominoes, lining up one at a time next to someone who has something in common with you. It might be something exterior (for example, wearing the same colour) or it might be something that both enjoy doing (like swimming). After each move, players talk about

why they were attached in that way. (This game is repro-
duced by kind permission of Joan Simpson, who invented
it.)   ●●●○**10**

Tag games

The wolf and the piggies   Choose one person to be wolf and provide her with a cushion. Play in a confined area. The wolf has to lose her cushion by pushing it onto a piggy. The wolf then becomes a piggy and the piggy with the cushion is the new wolf. The cushion must be passed onto the piggy's tummy so that they can dodge by turning backwards. With larger numbers there could be two wolves.   ●●●○7

What's the time Mr Wolf?   One player is Mr Wolf, standing at one end of the playground with his back to the other players, who are lined up at the far end. They advance towards him asking 'What's the time Mr Wolf?' His replies vary, until he shouts 'Dinner time and time to eat you up!' Whereupon he chases them all and the one he catches becomes the next Mr Wolf.   ●○○○6

Statue tag   One or two chasers, and when anyone else gets tagged they keep the position they were in at that moment. There are various ways in which their fellows can rescue them, the most altruistic being to take their place in exactly the same position; this also gives them a breather!   ●●●○7

Freeze tags   Most of these variations decide on a particular stance once anyone is tagged; for example, freezing with legs apart when their rescuers crawl between their legs to rescue them. Alternatively they can form a hoop which can be crawled through. Sometimes two rescuers are needed to join hands round the frozen player.   ●●●○7

Balance tag   Two players are chasers and they, as well as everyone else, have to balance a paper hat on their head. When a hat falls off the player is frozen until someone comes to the rescue and picks it up keeping their own hat balanced. Meanwhile everyone except the frozen ones are at risk of being tagged. If they are, then they become the chasers. At no time must anyone touch their hat to balance it or hold it on.   ●●●○8

Partner tag   In twos choose which one is to be chased by a third chaser. The other partner tries to prevent the target one from being tagged. When this happens the protective partner is now the one to be chased and the one tagged is the chaser. This can be played in groups of three making a triangle with one player being designated as the target by some means such as a band round the head.   ●●●○9/10

Maze tag   All except two players join hands to form a maze. The chaser and the runner cannot cross under the joined arms of the maze which has to be open ended. Either of them can touch one of the maze players on the back to change places with them.   ●●●○10

Co-operative rats

Argie Bargie Wargie   In this tag game pick a number of safe bases around the room. Only one player can occupy the base at any one time. When someone else wants to be out of the catcher's grasp they must approach a safe base and move the occupier off by the words 'Argie Bargie Wargie'. If the catcher tags anyone when they are not in a safe base they become the catcher.   ●●●○10

Co-operative rats   Two thirds of the participants are rats and the rest dogs that are chasing them. All the rats wear a tail which the dogs must catch. The rats try to stop the dogs from grabbing any rat's tail by intervening between them. Once the tail is caught the rat joins the dogs.   ●●●○9

Garden walls   One player is the gardener and stands on a chair in the centre with two dogs crouching at the foot of the chair. The four walls represent different kinds of fruit. When the gardener calls out a fruit, everyone dashes to that wall chased by the dogs. You have to join the dogs if you are caught before reaching the wall.   ●●●○11

Garden walls

Sing a song of sixpence In each corner there are four homes for the king, the queen, the maid, and the blackbird, each wearing a different coloured braid. The rest all mime the actions as they sing the nursery rhyme 'Sing a Song of Sixpence'. When it comes to the word 'nose', shouted in a loud voice, the four players rush out to tag them and bring them to their home. The first four tagged become the next king, queen, maid and blackbird respectively, until each player has had a turn at one of the roles.   ●○●○12

> Sing a song of sixpence,
> A pocket full of rye;
> Four and twenty blackbirds,
> Baked in a pie.
> When the pie was opened,
> The birds began to sing;
> Wasn't that a dainty dish
> To set before a king?
>
> The king was in his counting house,
> Counting out his money;
> The queen was in the parlour,
> Eating bread and honey;
> The maid was in the garden,
> Hanging out the clothes;
> When down came a blackbird
> And pecked off her nose!

Blind tag In a limited space the tagger is blindfold and counts to ten. During that time the players can run around in the space, but when the blindfold person finishes counting they must squat down and stay still. If they are caught they become blind and take the lead in counting and tagging with the first one clasping on behind still blind. This continues until everyone is in a long blindfold chain.   ●●●○7

Chinese touch One player stands on a rug or large square of brown paper and must not step off it. The others try to touch the rug without being tagged by the one in the centre.   ●●●○7

Escaping from the zoo The facilitator gives names of zoo animals in turn so that there are so many lions, monkeys, etc. The animals get together to choose a noise and action to portray themselves. In the centre of the circle is the zoo-keeper who picks four guard dogs, who have to go on all fours. The keeper is blindfolded as it is night. Then the keeper and the dogs walk round the inside edge of the circle and drop a bunch of keys in front of one of the animals, who stands and makes its noise and action. The other animals in that group have to run round the outside of the circle without being caught by the guard dogs before they get back to their place. If they are caught they change places with the guard dogs. This is quite a noisy game as the animals and dogs chasing them are all making their calls or barking! ○●●○**13**

French and English   Two teams line up at either end of the playground having placed a heap of belongings, coats, caps, bags, etc. at a certain distance in front of each team. The game is to capture the enemy's belongings without get-ting caught (and then having to join the other side). Note — this game has mediaeval origins which clearly pre-date the entente cordiale!   ●●●○**8**

Active skills games

Co-operative skipping   In pairs one player skips; the other runs in, they skip together a number of times and then one of them runs out again. They can also join up and skip with the rope held by the outer hands.   ○●●○**2**

Rope tricks   Two people are sitting facing each other on chairs several metres apart holding each end of two ropes one in each hand so that they are parallel. The other players take it in turns to jump in and out of the ropes, first forwards, then backwards. They can do a running jump two at a time over the ropes and back. Or they can 'jump through the window', when one rope is raised up high and the other stays where it is.   ○●●○**4**

Snake rope   Two at either end of a rope twirling it so that it ripples along the ground getting higher and higher. The rest jump over it in ones, twos, threes, and so on.   ●●●○**4**

Rope knot   For two players. A length of thin rope is lying on the ground: each player picks up an end with their toes and carries it to the middle of the rope. Then they try to tie a loose knot by working together with their toes. A simpler version could be a practice using one hand only.   ○●●○**2**

Grasshoppers   In pairs facing each other about 6 metres apart. One starts with two hoops and gets across to their partner by throwing one hoop and jumping into it and then repeating this with the next one, never touching the ground outside a hoop. Once they are together they both get back by jumping into the hoops together. This can also be played as a relay or as a three legged grasshopper!   ○●●○4

Roly poly bean bag Players stand in one or two rows depending on numbers. The first one rolls on her back with her feet clutching a bean bag which she passes over her head to the feet of the next one in line, and so on. When the bean bag reaches the end of the line, the last player hops to the front with the bean bag between her feet and rolls over to pass it over her head to land at the feet of the first one. This then can continue until they are all back in their original places. If there are two teams this can be a friendly relay.

○●●○6/12

Jumping bean bags The first player grasps a bean bag between the feet and jumps forward so that the bean bag is thrown towards a line where the second player is waiting. It may take several jumps to bring the bean bag to the line. Then they clasp waists and grip the beanbag between their inside feet and jump back to the original line. The second player then jumps back with the bean bag between the feet and reaches the line where the third player is waiting, and so on. This can be played just for fun or as a relay with another team.   ○●●○6/12

Wheelbarrows Couples are wheelbarrows: the one in the front prone with hands supporting her on the ground, and the partner holding her legs. Any of the circle games can be played with this position as long as everyone is part of a wheelbarrow: for example, *General Post*.   ●●●○10

Bar gymnastics With two people holding horizontal bars, other players can take turns in practising bar somersaults and various kinds of bar gymnastics.   ●●●○3

Walking wheelbarrows Paths are chalked out or long strips of paper are laid down which represent roadways through Yellowstone Park, which has boiling hot geysers that are dangerous to be as near as one never knows when they will erupt. Pairs of one small person and an adult make a wheelbarrow and they have to trace round the pathways without going off the track. If they do they have to wait there until another wheelbarrow rescues them by touching their hair. A more difficult version is to have the front of the wheelbarrow blindfolded. ●●●○4

Three-legged obstacle track In three-legged pairs, they overcome a series of obstacles, e.g. under a mat, over chairs or logs. A really difficult variation is to be in threes or even fours with ankles tied together, except for the outside ones. In the planning, it is necessary to be aware of safety and to have helpers at danger points. ●●●○6

Knots Three strips of material are held in a star by six people holding the ends of the strips, which are then wound into a knot without letting go of the ends of the material. Then the 'knot' is passed on to the next group and once again by holding the ends of the material strips the knot has to be unravelled. ●●●●12

Paper aeroplanes

Tangles   Everyone in a circle shuts their eyes and stretches out their hands to grasp other people's. Then they can open their eyes and manage to unravel themselves without letting go of hands. Sometimes it is necessary to swivel the hands round to manage this. Another variation is where two players are allocated to unravel them.   ●●●○6

Spinning a web   Take a large ball of thick wool and pass it to participants in turn who twine it round their legs, arms, or waists (not necks!). When everyone is caught in the web, once or twice or thrice they unravel themselves!   ●●●●6

Paper aeroplanes   Apart from the pleasure of making them, painting and flying them, they can be floated down from a height — a balcony or a hill. Each owner can see how far their plane can go: how many throws to get round the recreation field for example. In pairs you can get your planes to land together, then in bigger groups.   ●●●○2

Roly poly   The players lie down side by side in a row close together, rolling their bodies round and round. The player

Roly poly

at the top end takes the first turn in rolling over the rest and when she reaches the other end she takes her place alongside the rolling bodies and the next one comes down the line. Each one can choose the way she goes over the rolling bodies, feet first, head first, on the back or the front, parallel or at right angles to the rollers.   ●●○○6

Points down   In groups of six a number is called out and each group has to make contact with the floor with that number of parts: for example, 12 = 12 legs, 15 = 12 legs and 3 fingers, 4 = 3 legs and 1 finger with 3 people presumably carrying 2 between them and the other standing on one foot.
○●●○4

Pick and cup   The first player in each team is a pick, the next a cup, and so on, the last one always being a cup. The cups hold their hands in front of them to form cups with a fixed number of little objects in them: pencils, rubbers, corks, buttons. The first pick takes up one object and puts it in the cup nearest to her; the second picks up the object from the first cup and drops it in the next one, and so on down the line. Meanwhile the first picks have put the next object in the cup, so that all the objects are passed down the line one at a time. This can be played as a team relay or with just one line. Teams can be timed to see if they can beat their record.
○●●○6

Noisy pairs   Couples separate and when at some distance shout instructions to each other, such as 'Sit Down', 'Hop Around', 'Do a Somersault', depending on the ability of the partner. This can also be attempted non-verbally, in which case the game is called *Dumb Pairs*.   ●●●○4

Sweet in the bottle   Three players each have a string round their heads and another string fastened to it at their forehead, joining the other two strings at a distance of half a metre. At the place where they are joined is a further string a metre long which has a sweet tied to the other end. The game is to co-operate in lowering the string and putting the sweet in the bottle without using hands.   ○●●○3

Co-operative tins   Each person has one long stick or cane and they have to co-operate in stacking empty tins using the canes only.   ●●●○2

Co-operative logs   A couple has to lift a log over an obstacle. Each pair of players is supplied with one rope between them, which is all they can use. For the less energetic try transporting balloons with strips of cardboard from one place to another.   ●●●●2

Spirals   People are in a circle holding hands; one person leads off from one end turning in to start a spiral, and everyone slowly winds round until they are in a complete spiral. Then the leader makes an about turn and the group gradually unwinds itself. This is an effective end to a games session and can be accompanied by singing or gradually building up a collective hum getting louder as the spiral is complete, then dying down to silence as it unwinds.   ●●●○8

Seaside games   There is probably more co-operation in playing together at the seaside than anywhere else. Whole families are usually ready to join in throwing the frisbee, variations of tag, and building a huge sand castle. Here are two games specially good in the sea:
Launching the boat   In the sea or in the pool players make two lines facing each other and, holding hands, churn them in the water in an agreed direction. The end partners become the boat to be launched and together are propelled between the lines on their backs until they reach the end; then the next couple have their launch, and so on.   ●●●○8
Galley ship   As many people as possible sit astride a windsurfer board and try to get to a specified place by using their arms as oars in unison. If there were two teams there could be a boat race, making sure that the galleys did not collide. Unless this is played in shallow water the rowers should be able to swim, as the boards can overturn easily, adding to the fun.   ○●●○8

Co-operative balloons   Each pair has a balloon and two thin cardboard strips and they have between them to get

Co-operative ballons

their balloon into each of four baskets placed at four corners. This can be a friendly race or simply doing it for fun.

●●●○8

Hit the peg   This is a traditional game which has a similar counterpart in Bali. Players would carve their own 'pegs', which were rectangular blocks of wood, 20mm square and 100mm long, pointed like pencils at both ends. On each side of the square were carved the roman numerals I, II, III, IV, like a dice. Each one had his own peg; the first one would drop it lengthwise on the ground and tap it on the pointed end with a stick to send it spinning in the air. As it descended it was hit with a stick as far as possible, and the number on the 'dice' was the number of hits you could have for the next round. The idea was to be able to go round the block, seeing who could get there in the least number of hits. A co-operative equivalent could be to have one peg and take it in turns to see how many hits were needed to complete the course. These days 'round the block' would not be safe, so it would have to be played, with due care for others, round the park or playing fields.   ○●●○4

Dynamic triangles   Everyone is standing around in quite a large space and each one picks out in their mind two people who at present make a triangle with them. The idea is to try to keep that triangle, although everyone will have their own version of a triangle and will be constantly moving around. It is easier to choose just one person and try to keep the same distance from him at all times; in that case the title would be *Dynamic Pairs*.   ○●●○9

Co-operative frisbee   A group of players throw a frisbee to each other, but when it is caught the catcher has to be touching another player or be touched by one. The idea is to see how many co-operative catches can be made in a sequence. Later two or even three frisbees can be introduced.

●●●○8

Co-operative sports

Co-operative cricket   Everyone takes it in turns to bat and bowl and all the rest are fielders. To get the turns going, line up and count down the line remembering your number. Odd numbers bat first starting with 1 and 3 going on to 5 when one of these is out. Even numbers bowl first starting with 2, then after an over of 6 balls, 4 goes on to bowl at the other end, and so on. When all the odds are out, the evens start batting with 2 and 4, going on to 6 when one of them is out. When all the evens have had a chance to bowl then the odds begin with 1 and then 3, and so on. Everyone could get a chance of two innings to try to improve their score, as with everyone fielding there is a good possibility of a quicker turnover of people batting. Use some co-operation if the same number is called to bat and bowl at the same time! To make things run more smoothly everyone could have their number pinned on their chest.   ○●●○8

French cricket   Two concentric circles are drawn: one two metres in diameter and the other about 14 metres in diameter. Players are numbered off and number 1 stands in the inner circle with a cricket bat. The aim is to hit the legs of the batsman in the circle with a small beach ball or tennis ball. When this happens number 2 goes into bat, defending himself with a cricket bat. The first batsman replaces the fielder who has the last number. In this way by moving up in sequence everyone should have a chance to be in the bowling circle and then have a chance to bat.   ○●●○8

Three ball rounders   Five posts are made with sticks or clothes and the first one to bat hits three balls as hard as possible before running round the pitch. The fielders have to get the three balls into a hoop lying in the middle of the pitch before the rounder is made. Then the fielders take a turn to bat according to the number given to them at the beginning of the game. After batting they become fielders again. Soft balls, beach balls or tennis balls can be used.

○●●○7

Co-operative football   Three players in each goal and the rest trying to get as many goals as possible, first in one goal and alternately in the opposite one. Scorers change places with one of the goalies when a score is made.   ○●●○12

Balloon push   Divide into two teams and have two goals, one at each end of a pitch. As many balloons as possible are used and are distributed equally between the two teams. At the word 'Go' each player tries to pat a balloon into their opponent's goal where it has to stay. Only hands are allowed to touch the balloons and the great aim is not to burst any of them. Goalies will change each time they let a balloon through.   ●●●○12

Three-legged football   Two teams and equal numbers of three-legged partners. Each team tries to kick a balloon into the opponent's goal (a makeshift affair with clothes or sticks to mark the posts). If balloons are too expendable then a blown-up beach ball can be used.   ○●●●16

Six-a-side tennis   See how long you can keep up a rally. The side that has won a rally serves next.   ○●●○12

Handball   This is a simple version of netball. There are two teams and a soft or beach ball which has to land in the opponents' net, goal or even basket. The main rule is that no one can run with the ball and if the ball is dropped a member of the other team has a free throw. There are marked boundaries and if anyone sends the ball off, a throw is given to the other side. At the end the goals can be counted up, but the emphasis is on the co-operation in each team rather than a highly competitive structured sport.   ○●●○10

Co-operative squash   Two players hitting a ball against a wall counting how long a rally they can make between them.
●●●○2

Circle ping pong   As many people as can get round the table can play. A bat is placed on each side of the net and as they run round players take it in turn to hit the ball over the net and leave the bat on the table ready for the next one. As in ordinary ping pong the ball can only bounce once, but the new serve is started by the next one coming round on whichever side the ball has landed.   ○●●○6

Co-operative dodgeball   Two teams, one making a large circle round the other one. With large light-weight balls they try to hit the encircled team below the waist. Anyone hit goes and joins the outer circle.   ●●●○12

Seaside dodgeball   Mark out three squares in a line on the sand; divide into two teams with one in the centre square and the other team divided into two, half in each of the outer squares. With a soft ball or a blow-up plastic ball the outside teams try to hit the ones in the inside square below the knee. Anyone hit joins the outside team until everyone has been hit, then change over. This game can be played in recreation grounds or in a gym, but barefoot in the sand is very enjoyable.   ●●●○10

Piggies in the middle   With the same set up as the previous game, the outside team tries to get a ball over to the other side without anyone in the centre square catching it. If this happens the teams can change over, or alternatively the one who catches the ball can join the opposing side.
○●●○10

Back to back dodgeball   Form a circle with everyone's back to the centre and with one player in the middle. Those in the circle try to hit the one in the middle below the waist by rolling a soft or beach ball between their legs. The one

Running the gauntlet

who scores a hit replaces the target player. Alternatively the circle has to avoid the middle player, who will try to intercept the ball. There could be more than one person in the middle.

○●●○9

Running the gauntlet   Half the players are runners who have to cover a certain distance and fetch balls, one at a time, out of a box placed at the end of the pitch. The others line up on either side of the track behind the lines and try to hit them with beach or footballs. If a runner gets hit she joins the throwers. The end of the game is either when all the balls have been loaded at the other end or when all the runners have had to join the throwers.   ○●●○12

Balloon targets   One person has the balloon and tries to hit someone else with it. That person has to sit down on the spot, but can get free by either touching the balloon as it passes or by catching it. Before getting up to continue the game the sitter can free someone else by sending the balloon to them.   ●●●○9

Balloon targets

Look, no hands! The feature of this game is that no one can touch the ball with their hands. The players line up in pairs and the first couple raise the beach ball or football from the ground, carry it between them to an obstacle at the end of the pitch and get it back to the second couple in line, who do the same, and so on until the first ones are in front again. If the ball is dropped the pair should start again from the beginning line. This can also become a relay race if there are two teams.   ○●●○8

Wheel relay Four teams are placed like the four spokes of a wheel. The outside player runs three quarters of the way round the wheel and back to behind the last one in their team; then the second one who has moved up to take the first one's place runs round, and so on, until they are all back in their original places. Players could co-operate in that they should not pass each other, or alternatively it can be a team race. A good joint effort to end the game is to get the wheel literally rolling with each team keeping their line and proceeding clockwise as if they were spokes of a wheel. A call to go anti-clockwise could get the wheel turning in the opposite direction.   ○●●○16

Ups and downs   Everyone stands in a circle and the facilitator calls out a number with 'up' or 'down' after it. If she calls '5 down' there have to be five players squatting down at any particular time. They are allowed to stay down for up to a minute, but before that time other people will have taken their place so that there are always 5 players squatting, no more nor less. Then the game can progress by calling '3 up', or '7 up', or '6 down', and the solidarity of the group is called on to make sure that the numbers and positions are right.

○●●○8

Parachute games

Mushroom The most exciting thing about using a parachute is to see it hovering in the air above you as if by magic, before it descends gracefully to the ground. One of the simplest games is to have everyone holding it round the edge at ground level; then when someone shouts 'Mushroom', they all rise up to full height with arms above their heads to inflate the parachute. Players can take it in turn to call out.

●●●●10

Kangaroo Players call out all sorts of names of animals

Mushroom

while holding the parachute on the ground. Only when one shouts out 'Kangaroo' is the parachute inflated and there is a ration of one turn only to call out 'Kangaroo'. The same can be done with fruits and vegetables and then the magic word is 'Mushroom'.   ●●●○10

Mountain dome   Make the mushroom as high as possible by getting the parachute to be right on the ground and then with a sudden move right up to the outstretched hands. Then pull it down as quickly as possible to trap a mountain of air underneath it. Mountaineers who have been designated beforehand can then climb up the sides, which of course subside as soon as they are trampled on.   ●●●●10

Floating ghost   Get the parachute to produce a good mountain and then immediately all let go. It will gradually drift away as if it had a momentum of its own.   ●●●●10

Sky diving   A number of players go underneath the parachute and decide on a formation lying on their stomachs. The rest gently flap the parachute up and down giving them the sensation of floating. This is even effective if they lie on their backs, although this is less authentic.   ●●●●12

Sailing in the wind   If there is a strong wind blowing, the parachute can be made to billow by half of the players letting go and the others quickly lowering their side to the ground.
●●●●10

Name hooter   A hooter is passed on the surface of the parachute to a named person who then calls out another name for the hooter to be directed to. On receipt of the hooter the named played blows the hooter. This can be played with various musical instruments and to make it more harmonious, several being directed at the same time. All of the various name games can be incorporated into the parachute activities, for example, alliterative names, 'Jolly Jenny'.
●●●●10

Tossed frog   Use a toy frog or another animal cardboard cut-out or inflatable toy to make a storm more interesting.

Using the parachute start with a gentle breeze making the frog just move slightly, and work up to a full gale where it is leaping high in the waves. Make noises to accompany the waves and wind. Try making a whirlwind where everyone walks around in a circle while still wafting the parachute to make waves. Try making the animal do tricks or somersaults.

●●●●10

Cool frog Spread the parachute out on the floor with everyone kneeling at the edge. This is a giant lilypad with one frog sitting at the centre. At this point the facilitator goes to the middle, to explain through a story why the other frogs want to join the frog at the centre, but in order not to offend the rather grumpy frog in the middle they must ask to be let on in a particular way. Start a rhythm by clicking fingers or clapping and ask the question 'Hey, frog face, can we have a bit of your space?' The frog will then say who will be allowed onto the lilypad, e.g. all those wearing green can take one hop forwards. Hops can be forwards or backwards and using any colour, theme or subject. The aim is to get everyone onto the centre of the lilypad.   ●●●○9

Rockabye There are various ways of rocking children in a parachute and indeed adults are very happy to be rocked, if there are strong enough volunteers. The parachute can be folded in half or rolled up and someone can then be rocked to and fro as in a hammock. There can also be an inner circle of players lying prone, feet to the middle. They can be lifted off the ground gently and slowly revolved round. Alternatively one player can be put in the middle with the parachute lying on the ground and then lifted up and cradled; or she could be tossed into the air like on a trampoline. The favourite with small children is to have a ride, with someone dragging the parachute or spinning it round. Here they have to learn that the more players jump on the bandwagon, the less it can move.   ●●●●10

Earth and moon The parachute is held waist high and a large ball is sent round the circle clockwise; then a small tennis ball is sent round in the opposite direction. This is not correct astronomy, but it is very diverting especially when they collide. ●●●●10

Pop-up If the parachute has a hole in the middle, as all authentic ones do, several people can be underneath when it is held at waist height, and when their name is called they pop up and are greeted with a cheer. This can also be a name game: 'Hello Jolly Johnny!' or 'Three Cheers for Jane!' ●●●●10

Parachute hoop-la One person is standing underneath and the parachute is inflated; the players try to bring the hole in the middle over her head, down to her waist, then twist it gently round her, then untwist. ●●●●10

Mongolian tent When the parachute is inflated everyone puts their edge behind them and sits on it as the parachute comes down. If the players then lean back against the sides, it is like being in a large round tent. All sorts of games can then be played inside the tent. For example, the various cross-over games, including *Salad Bowl* and *General Post*; also the various circle games described in this book. ●●●○11

Monster from outer space From the Mongolian tent position everyone eases themselves into a standing position and then begins to walk, keeping the circle. It is worth having some spectators outside to see this phenomenon! To get synchronicity of movement there can be a director calling out where to go: e.g. so many steps to the right or left keeping the tent taut. ●●●○12

Pass ball A number of small balls are passed round the players who are holding the parachute at waist level. When a chosen leader calls out 'Pass Ball!' everyone helps to inflate the parachute and those holding balls have to exchange balls and places with someone else. ●●●○16

Tent pole In the Mongolian tent a centre person makes the tent pole in the middle. She points to one of the players, who has to get up and change places with her before the

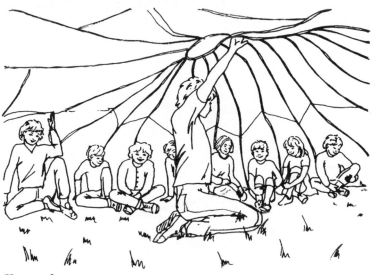

Tent pole

tent sags in the middle. The 'tent pole' then points to another player and so on in quick succession. Other circle games can be played under the tent: for example, *General Post* when the one in the middle calls out the chosen names of two players, who then have to change places without the 'tent pole' taking one of them. ●●●○11

Sunken treasure Collect the treasure in a box, either with participants or around the room, or connected with a particular theme. Place the box under the parachute, start some waves on the sea and send divers under to retrieve a piece of treasure. Can they find a piece that belongs to them, or something that they think they know the owner of? Or something small, cold, wooden or bristly? This is repeated with everyone who wants to be a diver until all the treasure is retrieved. ●●●○12

Poisonous snake The players hold the parachute at waist level and others sit or kneel beneath in the centre. A (toy!) poisonous snake is thrown into their midst. The centre play-

Big ball roll

ers do their best to shake it out of the parachute, whereas the outside circle are trying to keep it in. After a while new volunteers can go down to the snake pit. (The players in the centre can be on top of the parachute, but must remain kneeling while they try to get rid of the snake.)   ●●●○12

Big ball roll   A really big ball is sent round the parachute with the players controlling its course. One half of the players can try to keep it in the circle and the other half to send it out. A variation of this is to have a number of different sized balls to be sent out or kept in the circle, either with everyone co-operating or with half the players opposing the other half.   ○●●○10

Tossing the ball   If it is possible to have two parachutes, it is a great thrill to be able to toss a ball from one to the other and back. Rallies can be counted when players get proficient at scooping the ball into their parachute even if it is off course. All sorts of balls can be used, even several at once, or jumping 'frogs'.   ●●●○20

Cross-over   When the parachute is inflated with a count of '1, 2, 3, parachute!', the facilitator can call out instructions to cross beneath the parachute while it is still billowing: for example, 'All those who are wearing something yellow' or 'Those who had cornflakes for breakfast'. Sometimes everyone crosses, for example 'All those who like chocolate' and then the parachute has to be caught before it finally sinks to the ground!   ●●●○12

Snake dancing   Roll the parachute into a long cylinder and hold it over the heads of the participants, who then follow the leader in making a long line which curves its way like a snake, preferably to music.   ●●●○10

Fox and ducks   Several players volunteer to be ducks and go under the parachute which is held at waist height; the fox or foxes go on top. The sympathy of the players is with the ducks and they do everything possible to prevent the foxes from catching them, by making waves to hide the crawling ducks, who quack ferociously when they are caught! It is best to have a rota decided beforehand as to these two roles, as in my experience everyone wants to play both. Other predators are also used, for example, cats and mice; herons and fish; or swimmers and sharks. The group will try to help the mice, fish or swimmers.   ●●●○12

Crocodile   Everyone is sitting down holding the edges of the parachute waist high. In the middle is a hungry crocodile who 'bites' their legs and pulls its victims down into the river below. The victims let out terrific yells and get converted to crocodilism, attacking former players in the circle in the same way. This goes on until there is no one left to hold the parachute — they are all in the river below!   ●●●○11

Cross the lake   With the parachute flat on the ground, explain that it is a magic lake and its nature can be changed. With the magic word 'Shazeem', everyone pulls the parachute tight at low level. Then announce what the surface of the lake is like this time: for example frozen (quite taut), boiling with bubbles, sticky with slow undulations, or very rough with monster waves. Some players then have to cross the lake in a manner appropriate to the nature of the lake, with others left holding the edges to produce the effects. Repeat using ideas from players as to what the surface could change into next, making sure that everyone has the same number of turns to cross the lake.   ●●●○8

Roundabout   This is where everyone holds the edge of the parachute at waist height and walks around clockwise, getting faster and faster until they are running. Then they gradually slow it down until they crawl to a stop. Music can be added by singing or a group hum getting louder as the movement gathers momentum, then softer as it slows down. A parachute dance can also be invented with defined steps and rhythms like the traditional circle dances.   ●●●○10

Upside down ball pass   Make the Mongolian tent (see p. 106) by all lying on your backs, heads to the centre and legs up in the air to keep the sides of the tent up. Then pass balls backwards and forwards to each other, with name calling, or throwing the ball to be caught.   ○●●○10

Caterpillar

Push off   Players underneath the parachute try to push the balls that are circulating off the edge and the rest try to keep them on.   ●●●○12

Caterpillar   Everyone goes on hands and knees in a long single file covered by the parachute; they can then climb over obstacles according to where the leader takes them. They can be three deep and be tortoises in the same way.   ●●●○9

Pot the ball   Two teams range themselves round the parachute facing each other. Each team has one ball of a distinctive colour and the aim is to get their ball into the hole in the centre, at the same time keeping their opponents' ball away from the hole.   ●●●○12

Down the hole   Players are numbered off as fruits: apples, pears, bananas, oranges, to produce four teams. Everyone holds the parachute at waist level and a number of small balls are thrown into the centre, one for each member of a team. When a leader calls out 'Apples', the members of that team go on top of the parachute, catch a ball each, and try to get it down the hole first go. If a player is not successful the players holding the parachute shake the ball in. When all of the Apple team have had a turn they go to the edge and shout 'Apple!', whereupon everyone inflates the parachute and the Apple team retrieve the balls ready for the next team to be called.   ●●●○16

Games from other countries

It has been said that games know no boundaries and for all the games in this book there are similar counterparts in other countries. For example the simple game of cat's cradle is played the world over: amongst the Inuits it was part of the story telling with a different skill for each part of the story; in Ghana the string is made into a 'mosquito'; in the Philippines there is a mouse that can escape from the cat; in Papua New Guinea a fish spear is fabricated, and in Guyana a parrot that can fly!

There is the same universality with games with stones or marbles; 'Five Stones' or 'Jacks' or 'Knucklebones', with its complicated rules, can be found everywhere. In Botswana it is called Diketo and played with nine stones, and amongst the Inuits it is called 'Finger Bones' as they use the bones from the flippers of the seals. Skipping is a favourite and 'Jump Rope' from Mexico corresponds exactly to our jumping under and over the twirled rope and then performing all of the intricacies of 'Follow my Leader'. Tops are popular and in India children are very clever in keeping them spinning on their outstretched hands. Hopscotch was drawn out in the Forum in the days of the Roman Empire and then spread out all over the conquered lands. Hoops are often used for practice in aiming darts or arrows to pass through them as they spin past at great speed.

Besides these universal games there are many that are unique and highly complicated, requiring considerable mental and physical skills. In the following choice of games

I have chosen ones that are easy to describe, but a full range can be found in the books listed in the bibliography.

Takraw This is a game just played for fun in Thailand. The players are in a circle and one tosses a small ball (usually a hollow reed ball) up into the air. The players are not allowed to use their hands but must keep the ball in the air using their head, knees, elbows or feet.   ●●●○4

Whirl around This activity comes from Syria and all you do is bounce a small rubber ball on the ground and spin round once. You count up the number of times you can do this without dropping the ball.   ○●●○2

Dithwai This game is like *Know your Potato* and comes from Lesotho in Southern Africa. Each player builds a cattle 'kraal' or enclosure in the sand and puts his ten stones in it to represent cattle. In turns each one covers his eyes after having carefully looked at his stones. The other players take one stone each to mix in with their own 'cattle' and the game is for the owner to recognize his stones and take them back.   ●●●●4

Shash na panj This is a memory game from Afghanistan. A leader gives everyone a number and they all have to memorise their own and all the other numbers. The leader then calls a number and the one with that number calls out another; and so on. It must be a number that is being used and it must be said quickly. In this game ones who make a mistake are out, but it could easily be changed by making that one the next leader and starting again.   ○●●●9

Dodge the ball This is a Nigerian game very much like our *Dodgeball*. The players stand in a circle with one in the middle; in turn each tries to hit the one in the middle with a small soft rubber ball. If hit, the player in the middle changes places with the one who hit her. The object is to stay as long as possible in the middle.   ●●●○9

Kick and catch This is a Moroccan street game where two

teams stand facing each other and a referee throws up a ball
made of old rags into the air. Everyone tries to catch it and
gain a point to their team; they must immediately kick it into
the air again for the next catch. The rule is that a team that
makes ten catches in a row wins.   ○●●○8

Cover your ears   This is a Korean version of *Elephant and
Palm Tree*. The players sit in a circle and the leader puts both
hands over his ears. The one on his right has to place his
left hand over his left ear and the one on his left has to place
his right hand over his right ear. Then the leader points to
someone else, who does the same, with those to his left and
right covering their respective ears, and so on.   ●●●●10

Guli danda   This is a game that is very popular in many
Asian countries and is quite like the traditional *Hit the Peg*.
It is played with two teams, one batting and the other fielding. The guli is a stick about 3½ cm thick and 15 cm long,
with blunt points at each end. The danda is a strong stick
about 60 cm long. The first person to bat puts the guli in a
small hole in the ground so that the danda can get under it
and flip it into the air. When it hits the ground the player
runs and hits one of the ends with the danda to get it again
into the air, this time hitting it hard to send it as far away
from the hole as possible. The batsman runs back to put the
danda by the hole and the one who fields the guli throws it
to try to hit the danda. If she hits it, her team comes up to
bat; if she misses the other team gets a point. Everyone has
a turn to bat and has four goes to hit the guli; when the team
gets out, then the batting order continues next time they are
in.   ○●●○10

Tiro   This is a mixture between *Guli Danda* and baseball. It
is played in the same way as *Guli Danda*, in that it starts with
hitting the tiro (the guli) as far as possible; if it is caught or
if the fielder hits the home base with it before the batter
returns he is out — and so on with the whole team. Then
the other side bats. Points can be scored for those who did
not get their tiro caught or the home base hit.   ○●●○10

Guli danda

Clap ball This is a rhythmic clapping game from the Cameroons. There are two teams standing opposite each other about 4 metres apart. One player starts by throwing a ball (or orange or grapefruit) to someone on the other side; all the players clap as he throws, and when the ball is caught they stamp their feet. This is then repeated and anyone who drops a catch returns it to the tosser, who throws it again. It is said that no one wins or loses in this game; it is played for the joy of the rhythm.   ●●●●**10**

Numbers This lively game from Angola is very much like our *Huggy Bear*. The leader calls out a number and the players have to group together in that number; as soon as the groups are formed another number is called and they regroup.

●●●○**10**

Fire on the mountain This game from Kenya is rather like *Simon Says*. First a key word is chosen and then all the players except the leader lie on their backs. If the key word is 'mountain' the leader will shout out many variations —

for example, 'Fire in the forest' — and only when she includes the key word 'mountain' must all the players jump up; the last one up becomes the new leader.   ●●●○9

Pinata This festive game comes from many countries in Latin America. Everyone helps make a papier maché figure, bird or animal, which is then stuffed with tiny goodies, nuts, raisins, etc. This 'pinata' is then tied with a string to the branch of a tree. Each player then takes it in turn to try, blindfold, to burst open the pinata with a stick. When it is broken open there is a treat for each player.   ●●●○8

Help is similar to *Balance Tag*. It is played in Peru. When anyone is in danger of being tagged by the chaser, they can shout 'Help!' and if another player comes to the rescue and they can hold hands they are both safe. Otherwise the one caught becomes the chaser.   ●●●○9

Dakpanay Another chaser game from the Philippines. There are five circles, 3 metres in diameter, drawn on the ground in a circle. The players have to run round from one circle to another while the chaser tries to tag them. When they are in the circles they are safe from the chaser, who can only tag them when they are running in between. As usual anyone caught becomes the chaser.   ●●●○11

Evanema from Papua New Guinea is a real test of balance and trust. There are two rows of partners each player putting their arms across the shoulders of the one facing them. Another player climbs onto the arms of the first pair and walks along the arms. The partners first walked on then run to the other end to continue the walk indefinitely until the balancer falls off or gets tired; then the next volunteer has a go. It is like *Over the Rollers*, but needing great balancing skill.   ○●●○11

Networks The idea of this game from Zaire is to draw a picture or pattern on the sand using one continuous line. You are not allowed to take your finger off or to go back on any line. This is somewhat like our game *Double Action Painting*.   ●●●●2

Match my feet This is a circle game from Zaire with one player in the middle, and a leader in the circle. The leader starts off clapping a special rhythm and everyone follows suit. Then the player in the middle stands in front of the leader and performs a dance, and when she finishes the leader tries to imitate the dance. Then the leader goes into the middle and chooses someone else to imitate his original dance. Meanwhile the first dancer has started up the new clapping rhythm, so everyone has a turn as this pattern continues.   ●●●○9

Hit the penny This aiming game is from Brazil. A stick like an old broomstick is pushed into the ground and a penny put on top of it. A circle is marked out about 60 cm in diameter around it and the aim of the game is to try in turn to throw a coin at the penny and knock it off so that it lands in the circle. If you are successful you get another try.
●●●○2

Doorkeeper In this game from Afghanistan the players stand in a circle with their legs apart; the one in the middle tries to roll a small rubber ball through the legs of one of them. They try to stop the ball by quickly moving their feet together when the ball is coming their way. A player who lets the ball through can change places with the one in the middle.   ●●●○9

All of these games need practically no equipment and many of them are co-operative or have a team spirit and could be played in any country. There are many more games from all over the world to be found in the UNICEF publication *Games Around the World*. I am grateful to UNICEF New York for permission to describe these here.

Bibliography

Arnold, A. *The World Book of Children's Games*, Macmillan, 1975.

Asker, Carolyn. *Stories for Guided Fantasy*, & *Spirit of Fire*, High Warren, Barnet Lane, Elstree, Herts.

Bancroft, Jessie H. *Games for Playground, Home, School and Gymnasium*, Macmillan Co., 1909.

Beaver, Patrick. *Victorian Parlor Games*, Thomas Nelson Inc., 1974.

Bond, T. *Games for Social and Life Skills*, Hutchinson, 1986.

Brandes D. & Phillips, H. *Gamesters' Handbook*, Hutchinson, 1977.

Brandes, Donna. *Gamesters' Handbook Two*, Hutchinson, 1982.

Butler, L. & Allison L. *Games Games*, Playspace, 1978.

Cooper, E. *101 Games to Play*, Hamlyn, 1981.

Cooper, Rosaleen. *Games from an Edwardian Childhood*, David and Charles, 1982.

Cornell, J. B. *Sharing Nature with Children*, Exley Publications, 1981.

Countess of Mar and Kellie. *Favourite Children's Games from Around the World*, R. Drew Pub., 1984.

Daiken, Leslie. *Children's Games Throughout the Year*, B. T. Batsford Ltd., 1949.

Davies, A. *99 Games for Cub Scouts*, Scout Association, 1975.

Deacowe, J. *Sports Manual of Non-competitive Games*, Family Pastimes, 1982.

Dearling, A. & Armstrong, H. *The Youth Games Book*, IT Resource Centre, 1983.

Dunn, Roger. *Things to do With Games*, Macdonald Educational, 1980.

Fluegelman, A. *The New Games Book*, Sidgwick & Jackson, 1978.

Fluegelman, A. *More New Games*, Doubleday/Dolphin, 1981.

Frith, J. R. & Lobley, R. *Playground Games and Skills*, A & C Black, 1971.

Gomme, Alice B. *Traditional Games of England, Scotland and Ireland*, Thames and Hudson, 1898.

Heathcote, Dorothy. *Collected Writings on Education and Drama*, Hutchinson, 1984.

Hedges, S. G. *100 Garden Games*, Country Life, 1936.

Heseltine, P. J. *Games for All Children*, Blackwells, 1987.

Heseltine, P. J. & James, P. *Prince Philip Presents 101 Great Games*, Carousel, 1983.

Howard, Vernon. *Party Games for Everyone*, Blandford Press, 1961.

Judson, S. *A Manual on Non-violence and Children*, New Society Publishers, 1983.

Kay, Cornelia & George. *Giving a Children's Party*, Fontana, 1975.

Kohl, M. & Young, F. *Games for Grownups*, Cornerstone Library, 1951.

Kreidler, W. *Creative Conflict Resolution*, Scott Foreman, 1984.

Masheder, Mildred. *Let's Co-operate*, Peace Education Project, 1986.

McGovern, B. S. *The Playleader's Handbook*, Faber & Faber, 1976.

McKay, C. *Games Galore*, Scout Association, 1975.

McMullan, T. (ed.) *Winners All*, Pax Christi, 1980.

McToots, T. *Kids' Book of Games*, Beaver Books, 1982.

Michaelis, Bill. *The Family That Plays Together*, California Parks and Recreation, 1984.

Michaelis, Bill & Dolores. *Learning Through Non-competitive Activities and Play*, Learning Handbooks, 1977.

Opie, I. & P. *Children's Games in Street and Playground*, OUP, 1969.

Opie, I. & P. *The Singing Game*, OUP, 1985.

Orlick, T. *The Co-operative Sports and Games Book*, Writers and Readers, 1979.

Orlick, T. *The Second Co-operative Sports and Games Book*, Pantheon Books, 1982.

Parker, J. & Olsen, S. *Parachute Games*, Peace Education Project PEP Talk No. 17, 1988.

Prutzman, P., Burger, M., Bodenhamer, G. & Stern, L. *The Friendly Classroom for a Small Planet*, Avery Publishing Group, 1978.

Schneider, Tom. *Everybody's a Winner*, Little, Brown & Co, 1976.

Sobell, Jeffrey. *Everybody Wins*, Walker & Co, 1984.

Sternlicht, M. & Hurwitz, A. *Games Children Play*, Reinhold, 1980.

Storms, G. *Handbook of Music Games*, Hutchinson, 1979.

Weinstein, M. & Goodman, J. *Playfair*, Impact Publishers, 1980.

Yarwood, Richard. *Co-operative Games*, Peace Education Project, Peace Pledge Union, 1986.

Also by Mildred Masheder:

Let's Co-operate
This book contains many ideas for parents and teachers to share with their children. With sections on: a positive self-concept, creativity, communication, co-operation, getting on with others and peaceful conflict resolution. Illustrated with photographs and drawings.

1854250906   £6.99

Let's Co-operate Video
A lively and colourful video which illustrates many of the games in *Let's Play Together* and explores parachute games.

£9.99

Let's Enjoy Nature
A book to help parents, teachers and their children get in touch with nature and care for the planet.
With over 500 ideas for activities including: making things from nature; conducting experiments; growing plants; nature games; seasonal celebrations; exploring the countryside; conservation in the home and beyond. With 150 illustrations.

1854250922   £8.99

Freedom from Bullying
This is a practical book designed to help teachers and parents work with children to prevent bullying at school from nursery to secondary stage, and deal with it when it occurs.
Conclusive evidence shows that co-operation between parents, teachers and children can free a majority of pupils from a scourge that has plagued countless generations.

1854250922   £8.99

All available from Mildred Masheder at the address on the next page, or from good bookshops (except the video).

Let's Co-operate Pack

This pack is suitable for teachers and parents of children aged three to fourteen years.
The overall approach is experiential, with ideas, activities and games on co-operation in the classroom, the home and in the wider context of caring for the natural world.

- *Freedom from Bullying*
- *Let's Play Together*
- *Let's Enjoy Nature*
- *Let's Co-operate*
- *Let's Co-operate Video*, which illustrates many of the games in *Let's Play Together* and explores parachute games.

The pack is available for £50 including postage. Please send a cheque to:

Mildred Masheder, 75 Belsize Lane, London NW3 5AU
Tel. 020 7435 2182

Visit the Merlin Press / Green Print web site:
www.merlinpress.co.uk